W9-CXN-183

THE MASSEY LECTURES SERIES

The Massey Lectures are co-sponsored by CBC Radio, House of Anansi Press, and Massey College in the University of Toronto. The series was created in honour of the Right Honourable Vincent Massey, former Governor General of Canada, and was inaugurated in 1961 to provide a forum on radio where major contemporary thinkers could address important issues of our time.

This book comprises the 2014 Massey Lectures, "Belonging: The Paradox of Citizenship," broadcast in November 2014 as part of CBC Radio's *Ideas* series. The producer of the series was Philip Coulter; the executive producers were Bernie Lucht and Greg Kelly.

ADRIENNE CLARKSON

Adrienne Clarkson became Canada's twenty-sixth Governor General in 1999 and served until September 2005. She is the bestselling author of *Heart Matters: A Memoir*, *Room for All of Us: Surprising Stories of Loss and Transformation*, and *Norman Bethune: Extraordinary Canadian*. In her multi-faceted career as an accomplished broadcaster and distinguished public servant, she has received numerous prestigious awards and honorary degrees in Canada and abroad. In 2005, she co-founded the Institute for Canadian Citizenship. In 2006, she established the Clarkson Cup, which is now the championship trophy for the Canadian Women's Hockey League. In 2007, she was appointed Colonel-in-Chief of Princess Patricia's Canadian Light Infantry. A Privy Councillor and Companion of the Order of Canada, she lives in Toronto.

BELONGING

The Paradox of Citizenship

ADRIENNE CLARKSON

ANANSI

This edition published in 2014 by
House of Anansi Press Inc.
110 Spadina Avenue, Suite 801
Toronto, ON, M5V 2K4
Tel. 416-363-4343
Fax 416-363-1017
www.houseofanansi.com

Distributed in Canada by	Distributed in the United States by
HarperCollins Canada Ltd.	Publishers Group West
1995 Markham Road	1700 Fourth Street
Scarborough, ON, M1B 5M8	Berkeley, CA, 94710
Toll free tel. 1-800-387-0117	Toll free tel. 1-800-788-3123

House of Anansi Press is committed to protecting our natural environment.
As part of our efforts, the interior of this book is printed on paper that
contains 100% post-consumer recycled fibres, is acid-free, and is processed
chlorine-free.

18 17 16 15 14 1 2 3 4 5

Library and Archives Canada Cataloguing in Publication

Clarkson, Adrienne, 1939–, author   Belonging : the paradox of citizenship /
by Adrienne Clarkson.
Includes index. Issued in print and electronic formats.
ISBN 978-1-77089-837-0 (pbk.).—ISBN 978-1-77089-839-4 (html)
1. Citizenship. 2. Citizenship—History. I. Title.
JF801.C59 2014 323.6   C2014-902706-0   C2014-902707-9

Library of Congress Control Number: 2014938784

Jacket design: Alysia Shewchuk
Text design: Ingrid Paulson
Typesetting: Alysia Shewchuk

*We acknowledge for their financial support of our publishing program
the Canada Council for the Arts, the Ontario Arts Council, and the Government of
Canada through the Canada Book Fund.*

Printed and bound in Canada

For John,
Kyra and Chris,
Blaise and Tim,
Talia, Mylo, Theo, and Kai
with whom I belong

CONTENTS

CONTENTS

"With respect to what is eternal, there is no difference between *being possible* and *being*."

— Aristotle, *Physics*

CHAPTER ONE

THE CIRCLE WIDENS

WE ASSUME THAT BELONGING begins at home, in family bonds. Helpless as infants, we depend on family to nurture and protect us — we have the longest period of dependency of any mammal. Gradually, we become independent, learning behaviour and values from other people. In the 1970s, the British-American anthropologist Colin Turnbull published *The Mountain People*, a study of one tribal society, the Ik, that descended to appalling depths when their traditional nomadic grounds were severely restricted by the Ugandan government in order to create a national park. The work was later adapted for the stage by the English director Peter Brook. Both the book and the play caused a sensation.

In our benevolently romantic way, we imagine that members of this kind of semi-nomadic society are self-regulating — hunting, foraging, and sharing food and shelter according to perceived needs. We also assume that they would have close family bonds and would look out for each other with mutual need and understanding.

Indeed the Ik did forage and farm, but with their traditional movements and patterns restricted, the family structure and the foundation of their society soon collapsed. So distorted had the tribe's need for survival become that they could no longer uphold the values we consider human: caring for each other, sharing food, risking danger to save the weak, and, most important of all, raising children to adulthood. Instead, Turnbull revealed a society that manifested nature "red in tooth and claw."

In the pursuit of survival, selfishness became the norm and the search for food became the centre of the Iks' lives. Not only did they not share food, they searched for it alone, and they stole it from each other and even from children. As toddlers, children were thrown out of the family hut and fended for themselves near the outskirts of the village. When individuals found a source of nourishment, they ate in hidden solitude. If they found more food than they needed, they gorged until they vomited. They had become so consumed by their own survival that they simply did not care about wives, husbands, and children. Sexual relations more or less ceased, since producing children meant another mouth to feed and more competition for food.

The reasons for the decline of the Ik tribe were much debated at the time. Generally, the Ik seemed to demonstrate that the social structures, the family structures, which we consider inherent to human beings, were not at all necessary; the Ik seemed to be a people who could survive without the bonds of kinship, loyalty, and sacrifice. All structures and value systems can break down if their basis is severely limited, artificially restricted, and continually denied. The lesson that Colin Turnbull drew from the Ik forty years ago is the same one we can draw now: if we remove our sense of belonging to each other, no matter what our material and social conditions are, survival, acquisition, and selfish triumphalism will endure at the cost of our humanity. Under extreme circumstances, each and every one of us is capable of a mentality that brings about the abandonment of children, the lack of cultivation of human relationships, and the deliberate denial of love.

That our humanity can be lost for the sake of our survival is not a new lesson. The sacrifice of others in order to save oneself has been portrayed by artists like the nineteenth-century French painter Théodore Géricault, whose work *The Raft of the Medusa* depicts survivors of a shipwreck throwing each other off a raft in order to save the fittest. Starving and thirsty survivors killed and ate their weakest companions. The painting caused an enormous scandal at the time that it was first shown, in 1819.

It is society that makes it possible for us to develop ourselves as human beings. Personal relationships enrich us, work makes us feel useful, and goals give us purpose. We are part of a group, as we are all born biologically from a union. And it is as part of a group that we yearn to belong. If we concern ourselves with the idea that we exist because others exist, that we are in a web of human relationships, then we understand our individualism in a different way from that of the solipsist. Individuals are not independent of each other. We have individual rights, but we also have duties to others. But if we assumed that relationships are on a cost-benefit ratio, they would therefore be impermanent and fluid by definition.

In what follows, I will explore how a sense of belonging is a necessary mediation between an individual and society. And in belonging to ourselves and to our society, we have the greatest possibility to live full lives, connected to all other human beings.

ABORIGINAL CIRCLES IN CANADA emphasize that inclusiveness is a form of expansion. In 1977, testifying before the Royal Commission on the Northern Environment, Grand Chief John Kelly described how the Ojibway were cheated by Treaty 3, originally signed in 1873 by the Ontario government while the federal government stood by. Kelly pointed out that we work together by enlarging, by allowing people to join the circle, not by hierarchy, nor by sheer will and force of power:

Despite being robbed time and again by the government and more recently by industry, we still possess certain things of value which the white man covets. We have learned through the experience that wherever Indians possess or control anything economically valuable, there will be always those who will attempt

to steal it.... Each time [we are promised] per-
petual repose and gluttony... [we are left] with
famine and disease. It also appears that, as the
years go by, the circle of the Ojibway gets bigger
and bigger. Canadians of all colours and religions are entering that circle. You might feel
that you have roots somewhere else, but in reality, you are right here with us. I do not know if
you feel the throbbing of the land in your chest
and if you feel the bear is your brother with a
spirit purer and stronger than yours, or if the
elk is on a higher level of life than is man. You
may not share the same spiritual anguish as
I see the earth ravaged by a stranger, but you
can no longer escape my fate as the soil turns
barren and the rivers poison. Much against my
will, and probably yours, time and circumstance
have put us together in the same circle. And so I
come not to plead with you to save me from the
monstrous stranger of capitalist greed and technology. I come to inform you that my danger
is your danger too. My genocide is your genocide. To commit genocide it is not necessary to
build camps and ovens. All that is required is to
remove the basis for a way of life.

What we understand from this statement is that a circle allows everyone to see each other, touch each other, and lose fear of each other. The Other is no longer separate, no longer above or beneath, no longer unknown, but a part of the greater circle. In a circle we do not have to ask "Who is my neighbour?" because our neighbour is right beside us and across from us, and each of us just has to let go of a hand in order to let them in. In a circle we have to listen to each other's stories. In a circle we have to meet as persons, and we have to acknowledge that we share a culture or a heritage or even just the land we are standing on. And we cannot deny to others the right to belong. It is the most profound acknowledgement of our belonging to the human race.

As part of the circle, we belong to the same ring of being; we take our place and let others do the same. This neutral, unconditional acceptance is the basis of the kind of society we are creating in this country. Society, the network of groups, allows us security in numbers and a context for inevitable struggle. The joy of working with others should be in the effort of working together, not in the scramble to gain power, praise, or pleasure. Aboriginal life emphasizes mutual dependence, which is the ecology of human relationships. One form of life exists in relationship with all other forms, so that a bear or a salmon can become a human being or a tree. This is the most concrete and powerful iteration of the interdependence that we call belonging to each other, being part of a whole. The circle opens to include us, for better or worse. The circle implies a common fate that we share and that we acknowledge. Your destiny is my destiny.

EVERY SOCIETY IN ITS own particular way affirms the value of belonging in its history, its fortune, and its personality. Let me take you to a village I know called Eygalières, in the part of southern France called Provence, where picturesque ruins are surrounded by tumbledown walls, and a bell tower on the summit rises some one thousand feet over the plain. The northern gate was called la porte de l'Auro, which means in Provençal "the gate of the wind," and the southern one was called la porte de Sylvane, after a local celebrity. This latter gate had a somewhat sinister significance, because the walls on either side of it were drenched in a bright yellow stain made from crocus pistils (and therefore gave the street outside it the name it still bears today, rue

Safranière) to signal that debtors were not allowed
to live within the walls.

Although not spectacular in the showy way that
the nearby hill town of Les Baux is, Eygalières nevertheless gives you an idea of what it is like to live
in a high, protected place where you can see in all
directions. The village has a clear view of the range
of tiny mountains called the Chaîne des Alpilles,
which Henry James described as looking like frozen
waves cut into wedges of limestone. The peculiar-
ity of this land form is that if nothing were placed
close to it, it would resemble an enormous mountain range. The fact that it is miniature gives it its
charm and element of surprise.

For hundreds of years the village wall enclosed
1,400 inhabitants. From the eleventh century until
the sixteenth century, Eygalières grew by about a
thousand inhabitants, and these inhabitants shared
a rich history, moving from a feudal society — in
which all human actions, however small, were governed by the enormous forces of the Church, the
landed aristocracy, and the monarchy — to one of
relative freedom. As the village of Eygalières came
through the Middle Ages and into the modern
period, the people demonstrated their own power
by choosing for themselves how they might live

together and thus determining what it means to be an individual in such a society.

But to understand this passage from feudal duchy to "free" society, let's go back even further. Prehistoric remains of Stone Age weapons dating back to 3000 BC are commonly discovered in this area, and from a window of a house built into the southern part of the village wall, you can see a flattened space on one of the hills that has never been excavated but where local villagers have found remnants of the Chalcolithic Age. These are the remains of the Salyan tribes, of Ligurian stock and known today as Gauls.

At first the Ligurians established a civilization based on the *oppida* — city settlements on rocky hills surrounded by sheer cliffs. These fortified settlements were difficult to reach and were always guarded by watchmen. The location allowed for the safe storage of provisions, and the sanctuaries could be kept inviolate. The Salyans believed that cutting off the heads of their enemies guaranteed the tribe's protection, as the spirits of the dead were inseparable from their skulls. The wisdom of the dead was gained by accumulating heads. Many rocks in the area have carvings that depict decapitation. In some cases a carnivorous animal, such as a lion, is shown resting a paw on each severed head. The beast is not there to frighten his victims; he merely serves the sacred attributes the heads represent.

Despite all these safeguards against intruders, in 124 BC the Salyans were defeated in the Romans' relentless imperial march across the northern Mediterranean and into Spain. From the fourth century BC, the Greeks had penetrated the area, looking for water. They eventually found it at the Salyans' healing spring in today's Saint-Rémy, where there is an extensive Roman ruin called Glanum.

From about 100 to 50 BC, two important roads passed through this Gallo-Roman city. Vestiges of the roads still exist near Eygalières, to the north and south of the Alpilles. The northern road was called the Via Domitia. The southern road, the Via Aurelia, still goes through Eygalières. The town became extremely important to the Romans because of a spring called Aqualéria, or "place of the waters." An aqueduct was built from there to Arles, some forty kilometres away. Parts of the aqueduct are underground, where it can still, with a bit of excavation, be seen. The water flowed on towards Barbegal, an enormous industrial grain mill that used the natural slope of the hill to draw water and move the waterwheels.

The Romans established *silex* quarries nearby to extract the stones for the mill, and stones from these quarries were eventually used everywhere in Provence. For nearly two thousand years, stones were mined and polished here, and in the nineteenth century the industry employed more than one hundred men. Millstones with "Eygalières" carved into them have been found as far away as Russia, the United States, and Turkey. The weight of the millstones varied between 120 and 300 kilos, and the journey by cart to Marseilles, where they would be put on a boat, took two days. In an abandoned walled area just inside the southern gate of the village, one lone millstone survives, propped against a wall. How old is it? It is difficult to say. It could be anywhere from 1,500 to 2,000 years old.

But nothing lasts forever. As the Roman Empire collapsed, chaos subsumed the area, allowing other religions to make their hesitant appearance and bringing in cults like the Mithras. Visigoths, Franks, and other barbarians invaded, destroying the vestiges of Roman civilization. Christianity, which in the fourth century AD received an enormous impetus on the conversion of the Roman emperor Constantine, was given a terrific run for its money. Nevertheless, Christianity managed to

hang on. The religious orders established themselves in the middle of the malarial swamps, where
they managed to prosper and thrive by draining the
water and making the land habitable. The Church,
like everyone else, knew that wealth lay in the pos-
session of land, and in the eleventh, twelfth, and
thirteenth centuries, barons and religious orders
competed to gain control of the land.

It was at this time that Eygalières became the
property of a ducal family, the Guises. The inhabitants of the area around Bouches-du-Rhone (the
delta of the Rhone), in which Eygalières found itself,
gained the right to access the communal forest for
firewood and building supplies, to cut the marsh
reeds, and to hunt and fish. They were allowed to
graze their flocks from the middle of Lent until
September, and in 1242 landowners were forbid-
den to enclose uncultivated land.

The inhabitants also had the right to harvest
vermilion from the kermes oak, or *chêne kermes*
(*Quercus coccifera*). Female ladybugs attach themselves to branches of this tree and spin a web
around themselves in order to lay eggs. Women
and children of the area grew their nails long to
scratch off the pea-sized bug and its netting. Dry-
ing and grinding the eggs made a pigment of the

purest scarlet colour, known as *graine d'écarlate*, which would be used all around the Mediterranean to dye fezzes and tunics until after the Second World War. It was a very rich cash crop. The dye was worth one gold *écu* per ounce. In addition, all the villagers cultivated mulberry trees, many still thriving today, whose leaves were used to feed the silkworms that produced the silk for the lucrative industry in Lyon, two hundred kilometres to the north. So the inhabitants had ways to subsist and even earn some money.

The Reformation of the Church caused enormous conflict and bloodshed in the region. By the middle of the sixteenth century, Protestants and Catholics were seizing each other's property and massacring everyone who alternately did or did not believe in the authority of Rome. Women and children were rounded up into churches and burned alive. Still, Eygalières remained Catholic, even though many of the surrounding towns had shifted back and forth in allegiance, depending on which baron had power at the time.

By 1560, Henry of Guise was in desperate need of money and was persuaded to sell his village to the inhabitants of Eygalières, who triumphantly built a town clock to celebrate.

The interesting thing about this passage from tribal dwelling to Roman territory to feudal duchy and finally to "free" village is that Eygalières has an air of freedom about it still today. There is a kind of independence in the people that is remarked upon by other inhabitants of Provence. With the buying of their freedom in 1560 came a fundamental change in hierarchy. The villagers no longer had a liege lord; they were no longer vassals. On the other hand, they could not depend upon their lord to defend them in case of an attack. They were on their own. They had to develop other relationships. There had always been a government. There had always been a sense that the community was organized, and there had always been a merchant class because of the local millstone industry.

Right outside the north-facing gate was a hospice; now an elegant residence owned by expatriate English, it still has its interior fountain. Five kilometres down the road, Mollégès, celebrated because it was run by a convent of nuns, held the right of certain taxations on wheat and of appointing the area's policeman. He had the right to kill animals, and he was paid very specifically for his kills — for instance, for a partridge he would receive three deniers. The people of Eygalières took those powers back from the nuns but kept the privileges of hunting and foresting.

So what we have is a picture of an extremely organized society with an independent economy, the recognition of rights, and a structure that did not depend upon a faraway liege lord. With the rise of the merchant class came the rise of a certain kind of individuality, because money obviously became current and people were not just paid in goods or barter. What is also interesting is that while the villagers were exempt of any obligation to the Guises, they were still in some way obliged to the nuns at Mollégès. The vassals, of course, could have multiple loyalties and different commitments. But belonging to the Catholic Church meant they had a certain loyalty to the representatives of God's life here on earth — the nuns — and being of this world meant they were loyal to their superiors, the dukes of Guise, who in turn were beholden to the King of France.

In the Middle Ages, liberty was either a concession by the Church or an exemption by which a conglomeration was freed from serfdom to a lord. The fact that the inhabitants of Eygalières were able to gather enough money to buy their freedom is a sign of middle-class intent. It means they were able to conceptualize the idea of saving money, which must have been a completely foreign concept to many of them. They must have had leaders who considered this a good thing and were able to convince those hiding their money or withholding from church offerings that they should share equally in the buying out of their village.

So the people came together, organizing themselves into a group that was distinct from a household or a family and that had the common goal of living together in one territory, with agreed-upon rights. In this case, the territory was a village, and the people of that village decided upon their geographical boundaries and their right to live within those boundaries. The walls of the village marked the borders of Eygalières in a significant way. Some parts of the walls blend right into the cliffside, so that it is hard to tell where the cliffs end and where the walls begin. Towers and hedges were used to fill in any gaps. Those walls, hedges, and towers defined a space in which personal freedom was guaranteed. In the purchase of the liberty of the collective, some concept of personal liberty must have been at work as well.

The villagers belonged to an entity, which gave them an idea of citizenship — owning their own freedom, not being beholden to anyone outside their own territory, and not recognizing someone as their superior because of his birth.

During the Second World War, the village was occupied by Germans and divided between collaborators and resisters. Jean Moulin, a native of the next village and the man picked by Charles de Gaulle in 1943 to organize the Resistance, parachuted into the region and took refuge in a shepherd's hut owned by his family, one kilometre away from the centre of the village. He walked from there to Marseilles to establish the Resistance and eventually reached Lyon, where he was betrayed and sent to prison. There he was tortured and killed by Klaus Barbie, the Nazi commandant.

Some of the older inhabitants of the village recall the fear and food shortages of that period, and they can point out the houses where German officers stayed for three years. They remember watching the sky light up as the Americans bombed the nearby Avignon train station during the liberation in 1944.

Today, the road from the village in the direction of Lyon is marked Chemin de la Liberté, in honour of Jean Moulin. And the villagers are still very proud of Moulin, the hero who is part of them, part of Provence, part of France, as they have always been. He is part of their very fundamental notion of belonging that has continued to this day.

I've told this story of Eygalières to show how the human drive to create a common destiny is reflected in the idea of freedom and belonging in one small rural village. From the remarkable act of buying their own freedom to the landing of Jean Moulin, the villagers interpreted the meaning of their period in history — feudalism, the wars of religion, the Renaissance, World War II — and remained intact, emerging prosperously today as producers of apples, pears, and apricots for the European Union and olives for the finest olive oil in the world. Woven through the history of this small village is the inhabitants' ability to retain their integrity through the vast changes in their economy, the evolution of their relationship to the Church, and the loss and revival of their language, Provençal.

The village today still has three main family names, although their work as peasants, sharecroppers, and stonemasons has evolved so that they are now schoolteachers, landscapers, shopkeepers, and real estate agents. One of the town's mayors was a teacher of Greek at the nearby military *lycée* in

Aix-en-Provence; the son of the former post mis-
tress now designs and maintains gardens for the
growing expatriate population. There are elaborate
systems of greenhouses, and under the pressure of
the European Union they have replaced the intense
cultivation of melons with peaches, apricots, and,
increasingly, olives. The Alpilles themselves are
now a national park. Fastidious restrictions pre-
serve the historic character of every building.

But they have always been a village. They know
each other and they need each other, just as they
need their three cafés — one for each political ten-
dency. They are diverse, but united; they differ,
but they continue. They are Eygalièrois, and they
expect to be so forever. On the night before Bas-
tille Day, July 13, a communal dinner is held in
the village. The tables are set out on the street and
everyone eats a giant paella. When the dinner is
over, there's music and everyone dances; then each
person goes off to one of the three cafés: that of
the Right, the Left, or the Monarchists. The ten-
sion between the different factions is, in effect,
what is being celebrated. That the various political factions have different values is actually what
links them. Then there is a second communal dinner on August 10, to celebrate the Feast of Saint

Lawrence. This act of eating together twice a year, on the street, under the plane trees, is a continued expression of the communality of the villagers, of the way they live their lives. It affirms that they know that, despite their smaller differences, one large thing unites them.

SOME ARGUE, CONVINCINGLY, THAT this cooperative dimension within and among human beings is a result of the way the human brain functions. The oldest, or reptilian, brain keeps the chemical compound of the blood in balance, the breathing regulated, and the heart beating. This organ can still function when people are declared "brain dead." The reptilian brain also knows about aggression, mating, and even defending territory. But it does not have what we now think of as emotion.

There is a second kind of brain, called the limbic brain. The limbic brain is where the nurturing response to our offspring is located. As mammals, we bear live young and therefore have to defend and look after them. Mammals like us risk and sometimes lose our own lives in order to protect our young; a garter snake can watch without batting an eye as its wiggling offspring are smashed.

The limbic brain also makes communication possible between mammals and their children. There is vocal communication when, for example, a litter of kittens is separated from its mother.

The most recently evolved part of the brain is the neocortex. Speaking, writing, planning, and reasoning all come from the neocortex, as do sensual experience and what we call being aware, having conscious control of our movements. The neocortex gives us what we understand to be our will. In *A General Theory of Love*, authors Thomas Lewis, Fari Amini, and Richard Lannon put it this way:

> Many people conceive of evolution as an upward staircase, an unfolding sequence that produces ever more advanced organisms. From this perspective, the advantages of the neocortex — speech, reason, abstraction — would naturally be judged the highest attributes of human nature. But the vertical conceptualization of evolution is fallacious. Evolution is a kaleidoscope, not a pyramid: the shapes and variety of species are constantly shifting, but there is no basis for assigning supremacy, no pinnacle toward which the system is moving. Five hundred million years ago, every species was either adapted

to that world or changing to become so. The same
is true today.

Understanding that we have evolved to this
point gives us some insight into how our brains
have developed. But we can't afford to ignore that
every single part of us is still evolving. Because our
brains are made up of these three parts, we can't
simply direct our emotional lives or will ourselves
to want the right thing or to love the right person or
even to do the right thing, even when it's perfectly
evident. Our emotional life can be influenced, but
it can't be ordered around.

We can look at something like poetry as the
bridge between the cortical and limbic brains. Robert Frost wrote that a poem "begins as a lump in the
throat, a sense of wrong, a homesickness, a love-
sickness. It is never a thought to begin with." Poets
are the luckiest, he believed, because while many
of us are often unable to express what we feel, they
can reach for words and images that will represent
the feeling.

The animal behaviourist Konrad Lorenz was
the first to use the word *imprinting* to describe the
way that birds and mammals form attachments. For
example, a few decades ago, at the Vancouver Zoo,

penguins imprinted on their human keeper and dropped stones at his feet to establish the beginning of their mating ritual. The instinct to mate, which comes from the limbic brain, is so strong that it will fixate on whatever object happens to be familiar. Studies have since been conducted showing lambs forming bonds with television sets and monkeys with cylinders of wire bent into the shape of their mother. Imprinting shows that belonging is a part of our rudimentary nerve systems, our primitive circuitry.

Similar experiments have been conducted on humans. In the thirteenth century, the Holy Roman Emperor Frederick II, who spoke several languages, wanted to learn what "natural" language children were born with. He wanted to know if they might speak Hebrew first, since he considered Hebrew the original human language, or Greek or Latin or Arabic or the language their parents spoke. So he conducted an experiment in which a group of children would never hear any speech. Frederick told the foster mothers and wet nurses to take care of the children, wash and bathe them, but not to speak with them. In the end, the experiment didn't yield the desired results: all the children died having not uttered a single word.

What was discovered in this pseudo-scientific experiment was that human beings could not exist without the interplay that we think of as normal human contact — speech, gesture, and all the subtle dynamics that come through contact and communication. We have learned since that institutionalized children often do not develop normally because they do not have a strong connection with others. Behavioural studies have established that human beings who believe they belong to each other do not want to be separated. Whether a young puppy has lost its mother or a teenager has been jilted for the first time, the mechanisms of despair and protest are the same.

Even people living in groups develop a biological or chemical connection to one another. It has been documented that groups of women living together, such as nuns in convents or female students living in university dormitories, gradually develop almost identical menstrual cycles. We now know, through hormonal studies, the effects of pheromones on people. Not only are they powerful sexual attractors to the opposite sex, but they also have an effect on people of the same sex by coordinating their physical systems.

This mutually synchronizing exchange is called

limbic regulation. One would think that each body would simply monitor itself, but in fact the body is not what is known as a "closed-loop design." Human physiology is now recognized to be an open-loop arrangement, meaning that an individual's biological impulses do not seem to be completely self-directed. The babies studied under Frederick II are part of that open-loop physiology. And this means that even as we grow up, we continue to need a source of stabilization and confirmation outside ourselves. We cannot be totally self-sufficient. This sounds like heresy in a society that so values individualism and the self. But we need the stability we find only in society — especially in people with whom we have relationships. Those are the people who help regulate us, whom we can count on to stay near us, and with whom we can be "ourselves."

IN HER GROUNDBREAKING WORK *The Return of Martin Guerre*, author and historian Natalie Zemon Davis documented an intriguing adventure that bears on the question of the self in relation to society. The film of this true story captured the imagination of the public in Europe and North America for its insight into who and what we are, how we see ourselves, and how we see each other. The story of Martin Guerre exposed how societies often see what they want to see and overlook the inconvenient. None of us is self-sufficient; there is no true individualism, and anything that upsets the delicate balance between the society and the individual is enormously threatening to the social order. A society, in short, is an act of communal imagination. And belonging is the outcome of that imaginative act.

Set in sixteenth-century France in a village called Artigat, nestled in the plains between the Pyrenees and the city of Toulouse, the story is about a man named Martin Guerre, the son of a well-to-do family. When he was about fourteen years old, he married into a solid family that worked in tiles. The only problem was that Martin was unable to consummate the marriage. His wife, Bertrande, was pressured by her family to separate on the grounds of non-consummation; after three years, she would have been free to marry again by Church law. But she hung in. As Davis points out, Bertrande Guerre probably was not unhappy at the delayed consummation of her marriage — it gave her time to grow up and establish her identity as a virtuous woman in a male-dominated world.

After consulting a witch, who prescribed certain measures to be taken, and after celebrating four Masses at which they ate the sacred host and special cakes, the couple consummated their marriage, and a son was born. This did not make Martin Guerre happy. For reasons unknown, he left the village, after having stolen from his own father a small amount of grain, and abandoned his entire family. He went to Spain, where he took a position in the entourage of the Cardinal of Burgos, and from there he went into the service of the Cardinal's brother and joined the Spanish army. In the course of his adventures, he had a leg amputated, and his military days were over.

Meanwhile, in another part of the Toulouse region there was a young man called Arnaud du Tilh. He was a good talker and had an extraordinary memory. However, he became tempted by the ways of the world, playing cards, drinking, and consorting with loose women. He became a petty thief, and his restlessness led him to serve as a soldier for Henry II of France. Perhaps the two young men met somewhere between those battlefields and the areas around Toulouse. While Martin was fighting for the King of Spain, Arnaud was fighting for the King of France, and as the timing of their service did not quite coincide, it is hard to know whether they ever did meet. What we do know is that they looked alike, one being taller, thinner, and a little darker. Davis makes the very interesting point that people then were not as aware of their looks as we are, because there were no mirrors in any peasant households — mirrors were an object of luxury. The idea of the "selfie" would have amazed them.

The turning point in du Tilh's life came after he returned from his army service in Picardy. One day, he encountered two of Martin Guerre's friends, who took him to be the missing man. He was then presented to Martin Guerre's four sisters, who also believed he was their brother. Finally, Martin's wife was brought to the inn where he was staying, outside Artigat. Bertrande was uncertain at first, but when he reminded her of intimate details, like the white leggings that he had owned, she kissed him and said it was his beard that made him unrecognizable. Martin's uncle accepted du Tilh as Martin too. When he arrived in Artigat, the villagers welcomed him back because, as Davis says, he was back in his place.

The return of the new Martin Guerre is an interesting example of how other people create a context for a self. A Martin Guerre figure belonged in Artigat. If the villagers had any doubts, they silenced them because they needed him to be part of their society. But what is more interesting is Guerre's wife, Bertrande, who was complicit in the acceptance of the selfhood of Martin Guerre. As was later stated in his famous trial, surely you could not mistake "the touch of the man on the woman." But she and du Tilh even had two daughters, one of whom survived.

After her husband disappeared, Bertrande was neither a widow nor a married woman. By the laws of the Church, she could not remarry, because a missing husband did not mean a dead husband. Davis raises the intriguing possibility that Protestantism, which was on the rise in the area at that time, might have given hope to the couple by offering the idea that they alone were responsible to God and did not have to explain themselves through confession to a priest. They could also convince themselves that their life together had been something specially given to them by God. Perhaps they had even heard that in 1545 a new law was put forth by the Reform Church in Geneva, which said that a wife abandoned by her husband could, after one year, obtain a divorce and permission to remarry.

Gradually, things deteriorated. The new Martin

sold property considered to be the family's and then asked for an accounting of his inheritance, subsequently bringing a civil suit against his uncle Pierre. This resentment, which basically grew out of greed, worked on his uncle's mind. He became suspicious about the fact that the son Martin had left behind did not in any way resemble the man who now claimed to be Martin. Pierre convinced his wife and his immediate family that the man before them was not, in fact, Martin Guerre.

The extended family was divided, and within a year the whole village was divided. The dispute burned at a low flame, with families taking sides; Davis believes that the lines were also drawn between Protestant sympathizers and Catholics. And then a soldier passing through the village claimed that the new Martin Guerre was not who he said he was. The real Martin Guerre had lost a leg.

Bertrande and the new Martin conspired to make the story of the return hold. Then the new Martin was accused of setting fire to a neighbouring farm and was put in prison in Toulouse. Bertrande went to his rescue, declaring that he was her husband and that her uncle had falsely accused him because of the property dispute. The new Martin

Guerre was released on the charge of arson, but the uncle, Pierre, would not be deterred. Posing as an agent for Bertrande, he got permission to have a formal inquiry opened about the man calling himself Martin Guerre, under the pretext that he was a man of bad reputation and likely to flee. With this, the new Martin Guerre was imprisoned again.

At a certain point, the villagers of Artigat realized they were complicit in what was probably a lie, and it meant that they were lying not only to themselves but to each other, on behalf of one person. Depending on whether they were Protestant or Catholic, the idea that they were complicit in somebody else's sin of lying would have had different effects on their consciences.

As Davis points out, the new Martin did not come to defraud his wife or the villagers. He came to have a different life, to be a different person, to have a different self. The idea that he could assume another person's identity and behave with renewed integrity is what makes this particular story fascinating: it reveals how people regarded themselves as part of a larger entity. Yes, the new Martin Guerre was an imposter, but he honestly wished to create a new self, and he did it well. He made his wife happy and he was accepted by the family on an emotional level (after all, what got him into trouble in the first place was the economic question of his selling property considered to belong to the family as a whole). The real story behind Martin Guerre is the total desire to become someone else.

So how, in the sixteenth century, without photographic evidence, fingerprinting, or lie detectors, could you come to a conclusion about a person's identity? How could you know who really belonged? Only through evidence given by others and by the man himself: resemblance to his family; his verbal witness to his own life; unique body marks identified by witnesses. One hundred and fifty people came to testify before the trial was through. Nearly forty identified du Tilh as the real Martin Guerre, including Martin's four sisters, his two brothers-in-law, and a member of a very respectable family. Sixty-odd people refused to commit themselves, even though they felt that the prisoner did resemble the real Martin Guerre.

Meanwhile, Bertrande had to play a very clever game. She hoped that the court case would be lost, in which case her position as Martin Guerre's wife would be validated; after all, a woman's rights were tied to the rights of her husband, and above all she wanted to protect her son's inheritance. Her own reputation was at stake, the heritage of her son was at stake, and she did not want to be marked as someone who had knowingly lived in adultery. As a woman she declared herself God-fearing, a mother, and part of a family, which was a part of the village. She worked on her image as a woman easily deceived.

The new Martin was a star at his own trial. He had all his wits about him, whether describing clothes at his wedding or chronicling his activities in France and Spain after leaving the village those many years ago. His defence was simple: his uncle hated him because of the property dispute. Despite all the contrary evidence, the prosecutor prevailed. The new Martin was sentenced to be beheaded and quartered.

He appealed immediately to the Parliament in Toulouse, and at his own expense was taken to prison there. Arguments were heard again by the court; Martin's four sisters, who were considered to be "as respectable and honest women as there are in Gascony," insisted that he was their brother. Testimony that the new Martin had led a dissolute life played in his favour; since arriving in Artigat, he had been above reproach morally. Declaring a decision in favour of the defendant would, as Davis says, "give expression to the principle of Roman law that it was better to leave a guilty person unpunished than to condemn an innocent one." And it would have given weight to civil law, which in sixteenth-century France favoured marriage and children. Bertrande would have a husband and her children would have a father.

It was all looking very rosy for the imposter, when suddenly a man with a wooden leg appeared in the Parliament of Toulouse, claiming that he was the real Martin Guerre. News of the other Martin's arrival in Artigat had spread throughout Languedoc, the southwestern area of what is now France, and had reached the real Martin. Investigators had been sent as far as Spain to check on details of his biography, further disseminating the news.

Why did the real Martin Guerre return to declare himself? This is more than a question of identity: it is a question of an integrity of being that required him to be recognized by others. When his four sisters were called upon to look at the one-legged man, they recognized him, as did their uncle Pierre, the imposter's original accuser. When Bertrande came in, she was enormously upset, ran to hug him, and declared that she had been deceived by the false Martin Guerre. The real Martin spoke to her harshly, telling her not to excuse herself and saying that she had brought disaster upon their house. The court now felt it had proof for a definitive judgement. The false Martin was found guilty of "imposture and false supposition of name and person and of adultery."

Du Tilh's crime was more serious than fraud because it involved adultery and theft of heritage. So he was sentenced to death by hanging. He would then be burned, "so that the memory of a so miserable and abominable person would disappear completely and be lost." The punishment for the crimes committed is particularly fascinating, as it indicates that robbing somebody of their identity or selfhood was considered to be heinous. A friend of mine used to say, "I may not be much, but I'm all I've got." It was meant as a joke, but it is actually a very profound statement: our actual being, who we are, how we are perceived and accepted by other people, is all we have got. The judge and the court were recognizing this in a very profound way.

The judge, Jean de Coras, commented in his later account of the case, "In truth, there is nothing between men more detestable than feigning and dissimulating, though our century is so unfortunate that in every estate, he who knows best how to refine his lies, his pretences and his hypocrisy is often the most revered." The judge eventually wrote yet another version, which is more of a novelization of the story. He compared the imposter in glorious terms to Jupiter, who disguised himself as the mortal Amphitryon to seduce the man's wife. In this account, the imposter is much more of a hero — a kind of genius in the creation of a life — and in some way he becomes the virtuous one, because he knows how to craft his own narrative.

The lucidity with which the new Martin Guerre was able to assume ownership of the real life of someone else gives us an idea of how we can appropriate belonging. Everyone around us has a stake in our being part of the whole, part of the circle. He was a son who had to be acknowledged, a husband whose intimacies had to be validated, and a neighbour who had to be recognized. Whether we acknowledge it consciously or not, everyone who is part of the circle has a stake in it. The energy field of belonging is centripetal and magnetic, drawing us inexorably towards each other.

BEING RELATED TO OTHER people and living in common with them is what makes human life viable. Healthy people are not loners: even when they withdraw, it is to gain perspective from solitude, not to do away with humankind. In fact, necessary withdrawal emphasizes the need for others. Experiments done with monkeys have shown that total social deprivation destroys their lives and that erratic mothering creates vulnerability, awkwardness, and failure to attach. We often ignore this element in our makeup because so much emphasis is placed on our becoming individuals, with particular stress on competition and victory over others.

Thirty years ago, in *The Lives of a Cell*, American physician and researcher Lewis Thomas said: "Although we are by all odds the most social of all social animals — more interdependent, more attached to each other, more inseparable in our behaviours than bees — we do not often feel our conjoint intelligence." Now technology brings us into contact instantly through touching a screen. Perhaps the good side of technology is that it facilitates interdependence and communication over vast distances. But in some ways, this is an illusion of contact and joining and community. It is important to remember that contact does not mean engagement. Nor does sending or receiving a message indicate comprehension and understanding. We need to keep learning about how the attachment we learn as healthy, functioning human beings, from childhood on, can continue in a life dominated by technological processes.

I used to pick up a free Toronto magazine called *The Grid*, which had two fascinating columns called "Dating Diaries" and "The Hook-Up." The first was a first-person account of a date set up through an online dating site or some other method; in the other, people had applied to the magazine to be set up on a blind date. What was most wonderful and remarkable about these particular matchups was that the couple was not only frequently same-sex but also often black and white, brown and black, or yellow and white. Yet no comment about race or ethnicity was ever made by either party in any description of the evening. This could happen in no other country but Canada. All of these things — the open acceptance of difference, the ability to exist in the moment, the sense of crazy risk — seem to speak of an ability to have an instant connection. Perhaps, in that calm acceptance of the moment, there is hope.

It is, I have to admit, not a trust that I ever grew up with as a girl and young woman in the mid-twentieth century. Fear of the stranger, apprehension about sex, preoccupation with being able to

earn an adequate living in order to stay out of the
Salvation Army hostel — these issues coloured my
youth but don't seem to colour the lives of youth I
read about today. When I was growing up, I never
went out with anybody who was not personally
known to somebody my friends and I already knew.
I remember reading Mary McCarthy's story "The
Man in the Brooks Brothers Shirt" and thinking how astonishing it was that she could think
of meeting somebody, feeling familiar with him,
and even sleeping with him because he was wearing a certain kind of shirt. At that time, the world
of women was so much more constricted.

It seems there is a kind of fictive trust among
people today. The realities of Facebook and Twit-
ter allow people to exchange knowledge about each
other and therefore to exercise that sense of the
communal. In the past, people did not feel connected to each other the way they do today. We now
have many witnesses in our lives, but not many
witnesses *to* our lives. The false Martin Guerre
could place himself in the jigsaw puzzle of other
people's memories, other people's expectations,
because their interests were invested in him as part
of their larger idea of themselves and of the part
they played in the village. The people of Eygalières

know that they are bound together by their geography and their blood and everything they have lived through together for centuries. The circle contains them, just as they contain everything that has happened to them within it. Even when they fight, reject, or deny, they do it within their context.

The greatest challenge for us is to understand and satisfy both our natural competitive instincts and this deep longing for cooperation. It is critical that we acknowledge our existence in the context of other people. Life at its best exists in cooperative, sharing, and balanced relationships with other lives. This is the interdependence we call belonging.

CHAPTER TWO

THE GLORY THAT WAS GREECE

WHEN I WAS GROWING up in Ottawa, I attended
public schools that were named after the streets
on which they were located — York Street School,
Elgin Street School, Kent Street School. When the
capital came into being, the city of Ottawa was
chopped up into blocks and laid out in a grid by
British engineers. Everyone went to the school that
was in their neighbourhood. I would walk twice
a day, ten blocks or so each way, through winter
and summer, picking up my friends at their houses
along the way. The neighbourhoods varied: some
friends lived in houses, some in duplexes, and some
came from a part of town called LeBreton Flats.

On reflection, the geography of my public education was my first acquaintanceship with true

democracy, with what it meant to lead a democratic life and belong to a democracy. The way I
grew up assumed equality among us children. We
would all be imparted the same knowledge, along
with the same benefits that come with that knowledge. The fact that we might or might not have
meat every night for dinner, or only on Sundays,
was not material. We all attended the same school,
we all sang "The Maple Leaf Forever," we were all
examined for head lice, and we were all Canadians.

The other great democratic institution was the
public library, which, as though ordained by some
mystical heavenly hand, was at the corner of Lau-
rier and Metcalfe, halfway between Kent Street
School and my house on Somerset Street. For me, it
was like a palace, with its Corinthian columns and
Greek pediment approached by a set of wide steps.
This was the Carnegie library par excellence. When
I graduated from the Boys' and Girls' Library next
door and got my adult card, at the age of twelve, I
was thrilled beyond belief. At last I would be able
to take out six books every two weeks.

It was in this library, when I was in Grade 8,
that I came upon the novels of Gertrude Atherton
in the historical fiction section (Dewey Decimal
#813.4). I still remember picking up her novel *The*

Immortal Marriage, flipping through it, and wondering if I would take it home. When I came to the line that described the protagonist, Aspasia, as having "gifts of intellect that no woman in earth's history has ever possessed before," I knew I had to read the book. And within those pages, I first learned about how I lived in a free country, why I lived the way I did, what would and would not be possible for me as a woman, and where the ideas that permeated my day-to-day life in school and in that library came from.

Gertrude Atherton was an enormously successful writer of historical fiction, with particular focus on the ancient Greeks. *The Immortal Marriage*, which by luck or happenstance I picked up that fateful day, recounts the story of Pericles, the great Greek statesman and orator, and his companion, Aspasia, a beautiful and intelligent woman from the island of Melos. Unusual for the times, Aspasia was educated by her father, but also being a remarkable beauty, she became the model for Phidias' sculpture of Pallas Athena on the Parthenon. The statue was made of ivory and gold, and was the very embodiment of earthly and heavenly intelligence.

After the death of her father, Aspasia went to

Athens, where she became entranced by Pericles (who was married) and became his companion from 460 to 429 BC, the period during which he dominated Athenian politics. I have never forgotten Atherton's description of Aspasia's first sighting of Pericles on a dark night, when he was unaware of her presence. She described him as being "tall... helmeted and clad in a dark cloak...there was no mistaking that perfect balance and grace and awe-inspiring dignity." Aspasia was convinced that Pericles was the greatest man on earth.

It was in reading Atherton that I also first came to understand the democratic ideals that Athens represented in such large measure, and still represents to us in our modern world. I, who had been thrust out of my own world and taken to Canada, thrilled to the words of Pericles:

> We throw open our city to the world, and never by alien acts exclude foreigners from any opportunity of learning or observing...If we look to the laws, they afford equal justice to all in their private differences; if to social standing, advancement in public life falls to reputation for capacity, class considerations not being allowed to interfere with merit; nor again does poverty bar

the way, if a man is able to serve the state, he is not hindered by the obscurity of his condition. The freedom which we enjoy in our government extends also to our ordinary life. There, far from exercising a jealous surveillance over each other, we do not feel called upon to be angry with our neighbour for doing what he likes, or even to indulge in those injurious looks which cannot fail to be offensive, although they inflict no positive penalty. But all this ease in our private relations does not make us lawless citizens. Against this fear is our chief safeguard, teaching us to obey the magistrates and the laws, particularly such as regard the protection of the injured, whether they are actually on the statute book, or belong to that code which, although unwritten, yet cannot be broken without acknowledged disgrace.

Aspasia lived in a world where Pericles exhorted his people to believe that equality before the law leads to rewards based on merit and creates a society that is both free and law-abiding. All Athenian citizens, rich or poor, were full-fledged political equals. Democracy was not simply about laws or voting or constitutions; it was also a culture of values, hopes, and ways of living life. Pericles advised the citizens to acknowledge poverty and said that the real disgrace of poverty was not that it existed but that citizens would decline to struggle against it and eradicate it. He urged citizens to involve themselves in public matters. Those who took no part in their civic duties he condemned not merely as unambitious but as useless.

I learned later in high school and then in university that the democratic commitment to freedom and equality that happened over roughly two centuries in ancient Greece gave rise to political and consensual opportunities rather than limitations. What appealed to me when I was twelve still appeals to me today: that we belong to a society through the political equality of all citizens, not just those who have been fortunate enough to have good families, a decent education, and a nice place to live.

In Grade 8 at Kent Street School, we were not taught about the ancient Greeks and we would certainly not have been taught about a woman who lived out of wedlock with a man, even if it did happen 2,500 years ago. But I was captivated. I thought Pericles and Aspasia's relationship exemplified the most wonderful ideal of companionship, and I was swept away by the idea of this extraordinary woman who lived outside the norms of society. Her courage, intelligence, and daring character gained her the love of the greatest man of his time, and their relationship granted her access to the centre of a circle of great thinkers, people such as Sophocles, Socrates, and Heraclitus. No other woman had the privilege of sharing the companionship and participating in the intellectual jousting among these men. My twelve-year-old self revelled in the idea that a woman with strength of character (and some beauty!) could become fully herself.

Aspasia was always realistic and, in Atherton's words, she knew that

> she and Pericles must pass out of this benefi-
> cent world someday, their passion and perfect
> companionship done with forever and all that
> remained of their devouring intellects and radi-
> ant bodies would be a handful of bones in an
> urn....And that in due course he would go first
> was a thought she strangled and flung from her
> when it assailed her in sudden dark moments.

Aspasia's realistic assessment of her relationship to Pericles made her an even stronger figure in my imagination. She was a woman from history who made me feel that, as a woman, I too could belong to an intellectual world if I were willing to make certain sacrifices. At the time, I didn't question that I would have to make sacrifices. All around me were examples of friends' mothers who had obviously sacrificed. Their faces were often, as the novelist F. Scott Fitzgerald observed of women over forty, "relief maps of petulant and bewildered unhappiness."

Although Aspasia was not Athenian-born, and therefore would have been ineligible to become a citizen even if she had been a man, still to my eyes she belonged in that society. And of course I knew that women did not have a role in Athenian life. When Pericles addressed the population in the Assembly, he addressed them with the common flourish "Men of Athens." However, even as a child, I thought he meant that at some point they would be joined by women — they were already joined by one woman, Aspasia, though she was cloaked and disguised as a man. But what I drew from Aspasia's story was that an individual could find a way to belong, to overcome the biases and prejudices of her time.

THE TERM *DÊMOKRATIA* MEANS, literally, "people power." As such, Athenian democracy, as articulated by figures such as Pericles, seemed to be free, tolerant, liberal, and engaging. The Greek word for virtue was *arete*, and this quality was popularized together with loyalty, courage, honesty, eagerness to serve the state, poverty, and self-restraint. As Aristotle put it, democracy was "to live as one wants. For this is, they assert, the work of freedom."

One of the remarkable things about the Athenians is that all speakers and historians of the time emphasized that they were the freest people anywhere and that they were able to live their lives in Athens without being subject to anyone's orders. In Thucydides' account of Pericles' funeral oration to the fallen in the Peloponnesian War, Pericles says:

> We enjoy freedom in our politics and tolerance in our private lives. We are not suspicious of one another in the conduct of daily life, and we do not get angry with our neighbors if they live as they please. Nor do we convey through our looks that we are annoyed with others — which causes people pain even if it does not impose a formal penalty. We conduct our private relations without offense.

And this is the best that we have inherited from the Greeks: that we are able to have private lives free from constraints of convention and the pressure and expectation of others. It is only in private life that the citizen can become an individual and have a freedom of choice in creating a life for himself without interference from the state. The celebration of private life is the nature and the essence of belonging to oneself.

But once the individual acted in the state or for the state, he became an agent and defender of that larger body. In a way, the price of belonging to the state was that a citizen's rights could be taken away when the community felt that its status or its values were being threatened. Plato said with savage irony in *The Republic*:

First then, aren't men free and isn't the polis full of freedom and free speech and isn't it possible in a democratic city for a person to do whatever he wishes?...It has all types of constitution because of the license it grants to citizens... And what of this — isn't this gentleness towards those who have been condemned refined?... It seems likely to be a pleasant constitution, with no one in power, and beautifully diverse, distributing some sort of equality to both equals and unequals alike.

In other words, the freedom that each Athenian enjoyed was not an absolute right but rather a privilege granted by fellow members of the community.

This concept of the community being the greater good implied that the state's interest was essential to the interests of the individual citizen. As the Greek historian Thucydides said, "However well off a man may be in his private life, he will still be involved in the general ruin if his country is destroyed; whereas, so long as the state itself is secure, individuals have a much greater chance of recovering from their private misfortunes."

You could say that private life was invented in ancient Greece. And the Athenians were proud of this idea of the life lived by the individual, because it was based on the principle that all citizens had the right to be respected equally. The freedom of the person was interpreted within the polis as a democratic element of justice. It meant that each citizen had choices and a breadth of possibilities, but always within the context of what was publicly valued.

Athenian democracy allowed a good deal of

leeway between the virtues that were admired in public activity and the way one lived privately. Citizens were encouraged to take part in politics and in the military, but they were also able to withdraw from public life and live privately. This is what Isaiah Berlin has called "positive liberty" — the freedom and privilege to participate in the city's active political life and decisions. Most tellingly, this positive liberty was embodied by the question always asked at the beginning of every meeting of the Assembly: "Who wishes to speak?" It's a powerful question that has had deep resonance throughout the centuries, and it is the mark of all democratic societies. What is important is the *freedom* to speak, and the equity that that implies, but not necessarily the speaking itself.

When I was travelling in the Canadian North, I had dinner with a group of Inuit elders. In what order would the formal speeches take place? No one could say. So I spoke first, thanking them for their hospitality, and then silence fell as we ate our stew. Eventually, one elder said, "When we were hunting the caribou, I cut open the stomach and we drank the soup from the stomach." A long silence fell while we ate some more, and then another volunteered, "We haven't been hunting the numbers of seal that we normally get." And another silence. So it went around the table, everyone alluding to a different situation but no one spelling out a problem. When the Inuit are in a place where they will be listened to, and where they can speak freely — *both* being of equal importance — everyone will speak out, but only if they have something to say. They are not making any decisions and they are not asking for any promises; they are simply speaking.

Being there with those Inuit elders was a little like being in a Quaker prayer meeting: the silence, the spoken and the unspoken all heavy with meaning. The privilege of speaking is not one that can be abused. It is a gift that we in so-called developed societies have lost. In our Anglo-Saxon tradition, we think that speaking endows the speaker with greater value; we also believe that if you don't speak, silence denotes assent. For First Nations everywhere, nothing could be further from the truth.

THE FREEDOM TO SPEAK, and the equity that it implies, is the great marker of being a citizen. It has implications for society, the individual, and the very nature of democracy itself. The Greek historian Herodotus used *isêgoria*, which is defined as the "right of free and equal speech," as a synonym for the term *dêmokratia*. Herodotus tells us that it was through *isêgoria* that the Athenians

> increased in strength, which demonstrates that an equal voice in government has beneficial impact not merely in one way, but in every way: the Athenians, while ruled by tyrants, were no better in war than any of the peoples living around them, but once they were rid of tyrants, they became by far the best of all. Thus it is clear that they were deliberately slack while repressed, since they were working for a master, but that after they were freed, they became ardently devoted to working hard so as to win achievements for themselves.

Both freedom and egalitarian values were underpinned by the virtue of courage. Therefore citizens would be able to defend themselves by speaking freely, and they were also free to counterattack against threats from outside their society. This collective activity based on equality and freedom of speech ensured the greater principles of virtue, courage, and insight. Individuals were a critical part of the political process, so much so that citizens were encouraged to state their opinions even when somebody else had the floor. Everyone was free to speak in the Assembly in Athens; it was assumed that everyone had something potentially worthwhile to contribute and that they would do so to interact with other people, not simply as a demonstration of their own emotional capacities or feelings. Civility involved a form of healthy self-abnegation. In *Politics*, Aristotle said:

> Though each individual is not an excellent man, it is possible that when they come together they are better than the excellent types, not as individuals, but all together...For, it is possible that, in cases where there are many citizens, each one has a share of virtue and intelligence, and when they come together, just as the mass of citizens becomes a single individual with many feet, many hands, and many perceptions, so too does it become a single man in relation to habits of character and to intellect.

In other words, when we belong together, we are more than we could possibly be alone.

This model of democratic deliberation assumes that when opinions are valued and dissent is aired with respect, conversation can lead to truly democratic discussions and, ultimately, decisions. In Athenian society, confrontation, disagreement, and changes of opinion were central to the operation of democracy. In *The Immortal Marriage*, Pericles illustrates to the Assembly that if one is unable to explain their convictions with clarity, it is as though they have no concept of them at all. Criticism and dissent were not scorned, because they were assumed to be expressed with intelligence and respect, in which one person's place could be exchanged for the other's. Although certain philosophers, like Plato, believed in natural hierarchy, Athenian democracy claimed that the behaviour of ordinary citizens could be understood as embodying the wisdom of the masses.

This brings us to the necessity of speakers' having courage in the face of dissension. In the courts and the democratic Assembly of Athens, speakers were often heckled and shouted down. This was referred to as "disruption" or "commotion." Speakers like the Greek statesman Demosthenes would interrupt their speeches by saying, "Please do not raise shouts at what I'm about to say but listen to me and then make your judgment." Disruptions were commonplace, expected, and not to be denied. It wasn't enough to state your mind — you had to hold your ground and be certain that you could be heard above the din. This courage points to one of the greatest aspects of belonging to a society — the allowance for disagreement within it and with its leaders.

In Athens there was no long-term formal leadership; each speaker was only as good as his last speech, and he was able to perform as a leader only so long as people trusted him. And that trust resides, I believe, in transparency. Democracy, debate, the discussion of the public good have to be seen to be believed. And democracy is frequently a messy, ugly business. In our own time, it is fashionable to decry the verbal slugfest that is Question Period in Parliament, the unseemly brawling that passes for discourse. But I think it is important for people to say what they believe in Parliament — within the rules, but where and when and how they wish. I think it is a good thing to watch people being asked questions and having to respond to them. It is healthy to witness how people behave in these situations, whether or not they are well-mannered. It is better all around for us to see the issues being actively debated in Parliament, rather than just having it reported to us by the media.

Speaking out in public means leaving one's private world and entering the public one, which puts the individual at risk. The political theorist Hannah Arendt characterized this kind of courage as being "present in the willingness to act and speak at all, to insert one's self into the world and begin a story of one's own." This is not only an act of self-creation and individualism, it is a way of participating in the flourishing of society as a whole. If you have the capacity to participate in the world outside your private realm, you have begun to tell your story in a different way. This leads to acting in a different way, and acting, as Arendt points out, is never possible in isolation; to be isolated is to be deprived of the capacity to act.

Arendt goes on to say that conscientious action is the human being's exclusive prerogative, and, more importantly, that action is dependent on the constant presence of others. She emphasizes that we belong to each other; if we have no speech or action, we are "dead to the world" and we have ceased to live a human life, because it is no longer a life lived among other human beings. By speaking, and by acting, we insert ourselves into the world. Arendt says that "this insertion is like a second birth." We can only tell our own story (our way of participating in the ongoing human drama of life), and we can only learn who we are, or who we were, by knowing the story of which we ourselves are the heroes.

THE ATHENIAN IDEA OF civic courage supports the basis of democratic exchange and values that we still hold in high value today. At best, citizens belong to each other because they trust each other, and that trust is the key to all political functioning and fundamental to our modern notions of what a society can be. When trust has disappeared from the public sphere, just as it can from the private one, rot and breakdown set in. This notion of trust and belonging has been characterized by historians as lateral trust, which Thucydides again and again emphasized was the key element of the success of Athenian democracy.

But Thucydides also pointed out that democracies can benefit from some level of distrust of their leaders in order that the citizens not relinquish their power altogether. This kind of "necessary distrust" seems to have been the basis of the health of Athenian democracy because it helped ordinary citizens maintain power over a potentially self-aggrandizing elite.

While the Athenians acknowledged that there was an inequality of nature among human beings, they also taught us that all human beings deserved equal moral regard and a right to universal dignity. We can interpret the meaning of this notion of equality to mean equal political capacities and equal respect based on natural talents.

First, let's look at equality in terms of political capacities. This essentially means that all Athenian citizens could cast an equal vote in the Assembly, speak in the Assembly, and be granted the same equal treatment. Aristotle viewed democracy as a system of "liberty based on equality," meaning that citizens had the right to be ruled and to rule in turn, that there were no or minimal property qualifications for holding office, and that juries could be composed of any citizens, because all citizens were capable of judging the most important cases.

Then there is the notion of equal respect based on one's natural talents. Not everyone can throw a ball; not everyone can perform well on exams; not everyone can cope with children. But the best part of our society, which we have inherited from the Greeks, is the emphasis on what we can do as opposed to what we can't. In his funeral oration, Pericles pondered the notion of equality of opportunity:

Whereas before the law there is equality for all in private disputes, nevertheless regarding popular esteem the individual receives public preference according to his recognized achievement in some field — not by rotation rather than by excellence — and furthermore, should he be poor but able to perform some service for the city, he is not prevented by insufficient public recognition.

While in many ways Athenian democracy promoted a kind of equality that we still cling to today, theirs was not a utopian society. Slavery was legal, and women and foreigners were not given equal rights. Unfortunately we still do not believe that everyone is created equal. Some human beings are still regarded as more human than others; racism and bigotry persist.

Interestingly, Aristotle himself — who defined the term *polites*, or citizen, as "one who shares in the civic life of ruling and being ruled in turn" — was not born in Athens. He was a *metic*; that is, someone born elsewhere and therefore unable to become an Athenian citizen. One wonders if he realized how ironic it was that someone who was excluded would become a beacon of the Western tradition. So many paradoxes existed within

Athenian democracy, and one of the most telling is that the distribution of power very much depended upon the freedom of certain people and the disenfranchisement of others. For someone to belong, someone else had to be excluded.

Nevertheless, it is worth remembering that 2,500 years ago, an individual's ideals and his inclusion in a group neither oppressed his individuality nor encouraged him to be simply part of a group expression. The citizens in a democracy (excluding women, slaves, and aliens) governed each other and therefore themselves. For all its flaws, Athenian democracy still has much to say to us, and for that reason we cling to its components as if to particularly well-balanced pieces of an ongoing shipwreck.

IN THE ANCIENT WORLD, the citizen belonged to the city and the city belonged to the citizen. There were equal rights and obligations on the part of the group and of the individual. To be able to belong and yet able to criticize — to disagree, to withdraw consent — is quintessential to belonging, and it is a fundamental notion that has been carried down to modern times. But it must always be remembered that to subjugate all your selfhood, ideas, inclinations, and emotions in order to be part of a collective is not belonging. This kind of sacrifice to others in the group is conformity and, carried to an extreme, bondage. Belonging, in its truest sense, means understanding the nature of the connections between one another — the very nature of interconnectedness. It can never mean dominance or submission. To define belonging is to understand its laterality. It will always move horizontally and never vertically.

I no longer yearn for the Greek ideal that so captured me when I was twelve. I now know that its solidarity, its idea of the common good, and its patriotism were based upon the exclusion of women, slaves, and foreigners from political participation. We know with hindsight that the Greek ideal of citizenship was destroyed by Alexander the Great's conquest, and that the Roman Republic crumbled under the weight of its own longing for empire. The Roman Empire's disintegration through imperial dreams and monarchical megalomania is interpreted by historians as a consequence either of inevitable trends or of unforeseen accidents caused by human beings and their motives. But there was no question that in the ancient world, whether Greece or Rome, citizenship carried with it a powerful aura of governance, statecraft, and the negotiations we now know as politics.

Today we live in an era of globalization, in which national barriers are more fluid with the rise of interactive technology. But this new societal structure does not satisfy the human need to belong. Many people genuinely feel a lack of control over their personal and collective lives. While the nation-state is not a perfect entity, it is at least close to the familiar state of the individual — his home, the people he works with, the kind of traffic that he commutes in.

But the history of Western civilization has been dominated by notions of hierarchy and hereditary power, usually held by one family and passed on from father to son. In the Middle Ages, citizens developed a sense of self-government and a sense of identity that was very much linked to the rise of cities and to the relative anonymity and ability to accrue personal wealth that these new urban settings allowed. But citizens were beholden to one prince or another. Cities, duchies, counties basically were tied up in a network of allegiances to a lord, and citizens gained protection in exchange for their legal rights. Citizenship, which began as a means for ordering private and public life within the context of political organization, came to mean a trade-off between gaining protection and having rights. As we saw in the story of Martin Guerre, the citizens of his village had a vested interest in welcoming him back because he was part of the group, and their identity was part of his identity.

As kings established and expanded their territorial grasp and used their nobles to extend their power over more and more land, they were able to then promote the idea that they embodied a nation. In the seventeenth century Louis XIV, for example, was able to expand his territory to what we now know as modern France by asking his nobles to give him their silver, which he then melted down in order to finance his army. Gaining more territory meant gaining more people. And people meant power; people meant armies. When he was later successful in extending his boundaries and becoming the magnificent Sun King of legend, he repaid each of the families with gifts of blue and white porcelain made in China with their coat of arms emblazoned on them. Today there are families in the republic of France, with its vaunted ideals of liberty, equality, and fraternity, who proudly display this china in their dining-room cabinets in their chateaux, thus legitimizing not only their titles but also their loyalty to the idea of France.

This idea of the hereditary passage of power soon gave way to the revolutionary period, with the English Revolution, the American Revolution, and the French Revolution all occuring within 150 years. At this time, people used violence to free themselves from the subjugation of superior powers and thus become participants in their own destiny. But this period was often explosive and short-lived. The best example is the French Revolution, which culminated in the execution of the royal family and was followed within twenty years by the establishment of Napoleon, who reigned as a virtual dictator and then as emperor. This movement from a dynastic power, through revolution, and to the restoration of a more severe hierarchical power structure has been repeated too many times in modern history to consider it an accident.

The eighteenth-century Irish statesman and political theorist Edmund Burke noted that the worst thing that happened during the French Revolution was that liberty as social freedom became perverted. He thought that "liberty is secured by equality of restraint...another name for justice. Whenever a separation is made between liberty and justice, neither is...safe." For Burke equality was not the same as levelling wealth and rank. He cautioned that the creation of a new society should not be at the total expense of the old; he compared that idea to a castle that had fallen down and that might have had its walls repaired or had its old foundations built upon. In fact, he warned against building a society from nothing. Destroying the past, he said, meant destroying what was good with the bad: "Respecting your forefathers, you would have been taught to respect yourselves." This lack of respect for, and understanding of, the past was what he deplored in the French Revolution. In fact many believe, including many French people themselves, that the French have never recovered from the revolution, from the desire to totally overthrow one thing and then replace it with something entirely new, thus taking revenge on their past. It could be argued that the act of imagination that is needed for the ongoing creation of society is so badly interrupted by the bloody violence of revolution that the society never really does recover or find its way again, and if it does, it simply reverts to the worst excesses of the past.

The idea of the citizen, which came to the fore during the French Revolution, was that of the individual, as opposed to the idea of a human being as a subject to a higher power. The good that came out of the rhetoric of revolution was the idea of personal responsibility. It is this idea of personal responsibility that gives us our idea of what it means to be a citizen in our time.

In modern times the constitutional monarchy was established after the English Revolution of 1688. This form of government restored the monarchy while setting up a parliament that gave voice to, and satisfied the rights of, citizens. This became a modern replica of the Athenian model two thousand years before.

I have been using the word *citizen* as though it were the same thing during the reign of Louis XIV as it is now. But in fact the word came into being in its modern context as a result of the English and French revolutions, when the people became a power in and of themselves, without reference to any hierarchical or hereditary structure. However, they were not prepared for the consequences of overthrowing an order that had been in place for centuries, however shakily and however flawed. More than anything, the idea of personal responsibility entered into the consciousness of the people post-revolution and is still today a part of the consciousness of Western societies.

In Canada we understand what it is to have at

the heart of our citizenship an act of the imagination. We know that we can be citizens who are not related to each other by blood, religion, or even past history. What we believe is that we can belong to a country that has welcomed us and that fortunately has a very strong infrastructure of parliamentary democracy, common and civil law, two official languages, and an Aboriginal foundation. We start in this country not with a political status quo from which an idea of "citizen" devolves, but with an idea of citizen from which a nation evolves. This idea starts always with the personal question How do I belong? That is our revolutionary act: for the Greeks, if it doesn't exist on the ground, then it doesn't exist; for us, if it doesn't exist in the imagination, it can't exist.

It is true that the many levels of government within the modern nation-state — municipal, provincial, and federal — mean that our attention is equally divided and that sometimes effective participation is difficult and filled with stumbling blocks. People find an outlet for their civic duty by becoming actively involved in a specific cause, like saving a greenbelt or fighting fracking or speaking out against drunk driving. These causes can be more emotionally engaging for a citizen than political self-governance. But therein lies the difference between having influence and having power: governance itself.

Powerful commitments can be made when belonging is linked to sharing. When citizenship profoundly affects people, governance comes to have a greater and more enlightened meaning. A citizen who feels that she belongs has a true sense of equality that is based not on obligation or need but on generosity and the capacity to see and value the Other.

When nineteenth-century French philosopher Alexis de Tocqueville visited America in the 1830s, he questioned how ordinary citizens could be committed to a democratic project. He also made a comparison with his own country, France, which he saw as suffering from a malaise of isolation and apathy among its individual citizens. This, he felt, made them vulnerable to all forms of authoritarianism, and all citizens would be doomed to silence if social groups and associations bringing individuals together did not interact with public politics. What he noted was that the process of becoming a citizen was a gradual immersion and not a sudden plunge.

The Canadian writer Margaret Laurence urged

us "to feel, in your heart's core, the reality of others." I have always felt that there could never be a more Canadian sentence. One of the great values of belonging to any group with a purpose is that we act with other people, for the benefit of other people, knowing that we could not accomplish anything without other people. Thoughts and action have to be coordinated with those of others in order to reach a goal. And it is in these smaller groups, all looking in the same direction and defining friendship in the context of a mutual goal, that the true nature of belonging lies. We can't hope to recreate an Athens with the assumption that it represented a perfection of political activity and thought. What we can say is that it provided an intellectual ideal of democracy and equality that by striving and seeking we can aim to put into action.

CHAPTER THREE

THE COSMOPOLITAN ETHIC

IMAGINE THE SHOCK I felt when I looked at a document that was sent to me this year: a photocopy from a register in British Columbia's archives listing Adrienne Louise Poy, age nine, female, together with the rest of my family — my father, William; my mother, Ethel; and my brother, Neville — on the Chinese head tax registry. Having grown up and lived in this country since my family arrived on these shores as refugees in 1942, I always reviled the head tax and thought it was a part of history. While I always felt implicated by this law because of its innate racism, somehow I never thought it really applied to me.

My identity was first and foremost tied to my family. I somehow never felt that what was written about Chinese in Canada, and about the head tax, applied to me and my brother — the cherished children of two people who had lost everything and invested their hearts, their souls, and anything they could earn in our present and in our future. I belonged to them first of all.

Then, I felt, I belonged to my neighbourhood, my friends, and my schoolmates, first at Kent Street School, then Lisgar Collegiate, and later Trinity College at the University of Toronto. I never dreamed that I was a name in a ledger because of my race. As far as I know, we were never required to pay the head tax, even though it was not repealed until after we had been living in the country for a number of years.

Had I known then what I know now, I wonder if it would have made me feel that I belonged less to Canada, that I was less committed to being Canadian. I was part of a despised and rejected group, but I did not feel, nor did my family ever feel, personally despised and rejected. We were popular at school and at church. No one ever said, "You shouldn't be here." No one ever told us that we did not belong.

That was one paradox of being a Chinese-born Canadian back when we were a small, predominantly white country: it is not the laws that create how you feel about where you live and whether you belong; it is other people who make you feel that you belong. It is your school and your church and the people you meet in the park and have eye contact with on a bus. Then, of course, you participate as a taxpayer, as somebody who can enrol in swimming classes or join the YMCA. That is what makes you feel a part of your immediate everyday surroundings. It implies that we are citizens within the context of other citizens.

IDEALLY, WE BELONG FIRST to ourselves. If we are healthy, well-developed human beings, we become, as Carl Jung put it, "the person we were meant to be." In Jung's notion of personal development — of self-actualization, of creating and keeping a positive sense of self and an ability to have healthy, open emotional expression — lies the modern credo that we must live up to our potential, with all the freedom of choice available to us. Naturally, out of this comes the concern for our own physical safety, and that of our loved ones. We call upon ourselves to be responsible and to fulfill our duties towards those we love and those with whom we engage.

Next, as modern-day citizens, we believe in our country's values and we expect that our responsibilities will be equally matched by our rights, that our duties will bring rewards. It is worth noting that the motto of the Order of Canada is "to desire a better country." This motto indicates, with typical Canadian understatement, that the country is not a wonderful basket of goodies to which we and others contribute and draw interest from. Instead, it assumes that as citizens we are proud of our country and therefore we will help make it better.

I believe all new citizens must acknowledge that they are being adopted into the family that is Canada; they must accept everything. We are a country that has not dealt fairly with our Aboriginal people, that treated Japanese-Canadians with cruelty and injustice, that turned away Jewish refugees knowing that their religion alone could lead to their destruction. New Canadians must accept responsibility for these historical facts about our family. Just as in any family we accept that Uncle Harry is an alcoholic or Aunt Betty was a gold-digger, we say to ourselves, "They are part of us; we live with this reality." Citizenship is not a buffet where you can take the shrimps and leave the roast beef, have the chocolate ice cream and leave the custard. Citizenship is a fixed menu and we all dine from it. The food is given to us; the acceptance of the whole meal is our obligation.

A 1913 photograph depicts Scandinavian immigrants in long underwear and trousers with suspenders looking at a blackboard that states the duties of a citizen:

1. Understand our government.
2. Take an active part in politics.
3. Assist all good causes.
4. Lessen intemperance.
5. Work for others.

The injunction to help others as part of one's duty to one's country integrates a sense of place with a sense of self. We have interpreted citizenship as a consensual contract with certain emotive elements, such as a high regard for our natural surroundings, some respect for the institutions of government and the law, and, ideally, a commitment to helping advance the aims of our society in whatever way we are called upon to do so. Citizenship is linked on one hand to the rights of the individual, and on the other to membership and attachment to a community. At the very least, citizenship guarantees to the citizen a passport and a place in a territory. At its most generous, it enables the acquisition of wealth, social standing, and the ability to work with others within the context of an organizing principle established for the general betterment of human life. We still believe this to be true even though we are aware of voter apathy, terrorism, the resurgence of nationalist movements, the inability to deal with multiracial populations, and the despairing failure of environmental policies.

As citizens of a parliamentary democracy, we elect members to represent our interests and to do their best for us as a country. As Edmund Burke stated to his constituents

> Parliament is not a *congress* of ambassadors from different and hostile interests...but parliament is a *deliberative* assembly of *one* nation, with *one* interest, that of the whole; where, not local purposes, not local prejudices ought to guide, but the general good, resulting from the general reason of the whole...When you have chosen [your member], he is not a member of Bristol, but he is a member of *parliament*.

In many ways, our parliamentary democracy idealizes the concept embodied by the Althing, the great assembly of Icelandic chieftains that formed in 930 AD and continued for two hundred years. The Althing held an annual meeting for two weeks in June, at the time of the summer solstice, when the weather was good. All the chieftains of the land gathered not only to make laws but to share gossip, buy and sell goods and merchandise, and even do some matchmaking. They converged on the banks of the Axe River, a site known as Thingvellir. For those two weeks, Thingvellir became the nation's capital. Friendships and love affairs were initiated or continued; all citizens saw each other face to face, and promises were made. New laws were enacted and old ones were reviewed. Everything was done in the open air and in public. The context of this superb democratic government was its location: a huge island of incredible natural beauty that had no need of defence with its difficult rocky shore-line, volcanoes, interior desert, and minute, scattered population. In fact, there was no need for any executive powers to be exercised by anyone. The Althing confirmed and secured the rights of the chieftains, who represented all the small communities. The mixture of formality — lawmaking and revision — and a fair-like atmosphere made for a kind of direct contact between the chieftains and the people, that only a small population on an isolated piece of land could enjoy.

In many ways, this represents the democratic ideals that we still hold. The Icelanders belonged to their small group that had settled the island several centuries before. Although they were once believed to have descended from Vikings in Norway, the most recent genetic studies have uncovered some extraordinary facts: the genetic roots of 80 percent of Icelandic men can be traced to Norway, but 60 percent of the women have genetic roots in Britain, mostly from the Scottish islands. In order to build their country and to inhabit their land, the Icelandic men raided Ireland and the Scottish islands and brought the women back. The Icelanders are very proud of who they are and from whom they descend. Until recently, the phone book listed people's given names first, and then their last names, which consisted of one parent's name and the suffix *dottir* (daughter) or *sson* (son). It was only when they emigrated to places like Canada that the people adopted and stuck with one surname through the generations. Still today, many people in Iceland have their exact identity within their generation indicated by suffixes. They are very proud of their family lineage and, by implication, the sense of belonging to their country. The Icelanders are an example of naturally rooted patriotism. They are quite simply, and demonstrably, one family.

THERE IS NO DOUBT that the fullest expression of citizenship requires a guarantee of civil, political, and social rights so that everyone feels they are part of the society and can enjoy everything the society has to offer. If any of these rights are withheld, the individual feels, quite rightly, excluded. This view of citizenship, of course, enforces entitlements that belong to the citizen even if he never exercises his right to participate in public life. Citizens, if they do not want to participate positively, nevertheless have to be loyal, law-abiding, and able to work. They must have the capacity to respect the rights of others. And they must have the ability to evaluate those who hold public office — this allows them to perform the minimum civic duty, which is to vote. In our modern pluralistic, diverse societies, citizens who want to be active must develop in a muscular way the ability to respond to realities of racial, social, and religious diversity in a situation far removed from the ideal realm of the Athenian city-state.

One of the most important aspects of this kind of civic participation in our modern life is the ability to take part in public discourse. As we saw in the previous chapter, public discourse has its roots in the Assembly, where Athenians were able to speak out, and even shout out, their opinions and their arguments about how to better their society. Now we do it by voting for representatives who are supposed to be governing in our name.

Listening to other people's ideas, even if they have been elected by us, is not always something we want to do; often we find their ideas unlikeable, even weird, and from time to time difficult to accept. But the essence of a citizen's participation is the ability to engage in a conversation with others, and with those we elect to represent us, in order to understand their position and respond respectfully, even if forcefully — but always to carry on the conversation. This kind of engagement is the opposite of inert acceptance or, even worse, of everybody taking their turn to have their own way. If we are to be involved in healthy self-governance as citizens, we must listen, but we also must know that we are listened to. The same rules that apply to any civilized discourse must be exercised in the democratic conversation among citizens. People need to provide reasons for making political demands, and these demands cannot simply be whimsical or threatening. Knowing and acknowledging that other citizens exist, that they are legitimate, has to enter this reality so that an individual is able to state her views such that she will be understood and accepted by people of completely different backgrounds.

In a country like Canada, this last point is particularly important. It is useful here to invoke a phrase that was first used by His Highness the Aga Khan, the spiritual leader of Ismailis, as a way of interpreting our ability to approach the world with all of its inherent complexity: he posits the need for a "cosmopolitan ethic." This is an elegant way of stating the need to engage in a conversation with another citizen whose background, loyalties, religion, and ethnicity may be completely different from yours. This kind of discourse requires considerable effort, continuing education, and thoughtful sensitivity. But it is the only way in which we can discern the difference between personal beliefs and public engagement.

In this way, I believe that a modern democracy can offer its citizens the ability to enrich their lives personally through public engagement. The private life does not require the same adjustments, because people seek people who are of like minds, who have the same experiences, who travel to the same destinations. There is an enormous comfort in dealing with them, because so much can go unsaid. But in a society of difference and plurality, that comfort does not exist. Every single step we take, every decision that we are required to make, will result in some level of discomfort. Democracy today is very tiring. The only way not to be exhausted by the process is to be agile in dealing with the matters that will inevitably enter the public sphere from the private.

So it is critical when dealing with questions relating to governance and rights that people are engaged in the exact moment of history in which they are living. I remember the rise of the second wave of feminism in the seventies, when it was suggested that the laws of abortion should be decided only by women, since it is women who give birth. The problem with that position is that the rest of society, i.e., men, also has a deep interest in the issue. The bodies of women are still the only reproductive vehicles available to us, at least for now. Would one let the rights of women trump what some would say were the rights of the continuation of the human race? Although arguments like this may sound absurd, they train our minds to deal with the questions that will come hurtling down at us through technological change. These are the kinds of questions that we do not want to deal with as citizens, because they delve into deeply held beliefs, or even ingrained prejudices.

There is no question that we have to demand more of each other as citizens. We must, like the Athenians, be able to speak out, criticize authority, and be identified as doing so. But we must also seek mutual understanding through conversation, deliberation, and simply hearing out the other person. This must be done without threats or cajoling, and most important of all with a properly guarded need for personal benefit.

Unfortunately, this kind of participatory conversation, of speaking and listening, does not jibe with the current trends in people's commitment to political participation. Not only that, but many people do not pay good critical attention to what their governments do, nor do they seek to have these conversations. The regard for such civic participation is on the decline. Indifferent passivity is the trend now. Today, people who have the privilege to vote seem to care less, vote less, and be less critical, in the true sense of that word, of their leaders and institutions than at any other time in history. We criticize, but we are not critical.

In the nineteenth century, the Swiss politician Benjamin Constant wrote that people actually gain freedom through the act of participating in political power, not by simply seeking unimpeded personal well-being, pleasure, and relationships. In the Athenian world, citizens felt they belonged to their state by sacrificing private liberty to promote public life. It is interesting to note that when someone exits a position of power, political or economic, they often state that they are leaving for personal reasons, to "spend more time with their family." We have all come to know what that means.

True privacy for the citizen means freedom from interference by public officials. A private life means we do not have to fear surveillance by the state. A private life means the ability to create passionate relationships and idiosyncratic associations. Groups can be formed to give individual citizens a wider collective voice to state private wishes and gain access to public officials. If a private life is considered more meaningful than a public one, it is because we can effect change in it more quickly. Intimacy provides love, and personal respect provides more affirmation to us as human beings than life in a public sphere, where there is deliberate misrepresentation of one's goals and where cupidity can play a huge role. There is no question that for an ordinary citizen to consider an all-encompassing political life, the word *sacrifice* comes to mind instantly. If all public life and public participation becomes a matter of sacrifice, it goes without saying that people will not want to participate. And it is necessary for average citizens to mobilize in whatever way they can to participate in the political process.

It is evident now that the idea of Athenian democracy simply wouldn't work, even if we broke ourselves down into small groups and had forums in which to express ourselves and develop ideas that might influence our political parties. In a modern world where private life is engaging, enriching, and completely self-sustaining, it is difficult to persuade people to take part in public life. Also, in a society of diversity and difference, we cannot expect people to have a singular idea of the common good. The Socratic reflection that "the unexamined life is not worth living" is no longer accepted by every-one. Such an idea of reflection on the whole of life is anathema to anyone who considers Hell not to be other people, as Jean-Paul Sartre said it was, but just being alone on a Saturday night. Many people living very satisfying lives, and even seemingly socially productive ones, are selective solipsists.

I had a memorable conversation with someone on a beach in the Caribbean who asked me, "Do you ever read?" I enjoy this kind of interchange with strangers, and I said to him, "From time to time." He smiled broadly and said, "A woman after my own heart! I don't believe in reading. It fills your head with ideas and makes you think too much." When I meet somebody like that, I think grimly to myself that a good state cannot function without good citizens, in the active sense of that word. Without every citizen's active participation in maintaining the public good, society cannot be expected to sustain the same benefits and freedoms. Passivity or minimalism is a kind of libertarianism carried to its extremes — non-interference with others and following only the most basic rules of law. Without participation, our society will not progress. We will lose all sense of being a civil society.

WHAT IS IT THAT we get from others? The whole function and idea of democracy lies within each of us and our ability to accept and include the Other. This is the cosmopolitan ethic. We have obligations as citizens not just towards the state and its institutions but towards each other as individuals and as equal citizens. One who does not behave in this way betrays his own citizenship. For us to function as a truly democratic society, we must be civil with each other and treat each other with the respect that is due. If somebody suffers from discrimination on the basis of race or religion or sexual orientation, she is being denied her true citizenship by her fellow citizens, even if it is not the state that is discriminating against her.

Those who live lawfully among us, whatever the technical status the state has accorded them — citizen, permanent resident, temporary visitor, or refugee — deserve the equity and compassion that will allow them to live healthy lives dignified by respect and consideration. For example, health is a fundamental human right and is important to being a productive citizen. We need to ensure that it is available to everyone in our country. If we exclude any person whose legal status guarantees them a place in society, we are violating our own values, undermining our own decency, and ultimately working against our own well-being.

It is very important that civility, which critics equate with hypocrisy, is not neglected. There is a heart of darkness in every human being. The measure of a civilized society is not restraint through law but behaviour through custom. I do not believe that human nature can be transformed or that human beings can be made better at heart. Human nature is what it is. But I do believe that conditions protecting human life and dignity can encourage and sustain people in doing the right thing. In his essay "Education for Citizenship," the political philosopher Will Kymlicka points out the difference between the "moral obligation of civility" and "an aesthetic conception of good manners." Civility is reciprocal; it means doing unto others as you would have them do unto you.

So how do we foster the ability to act in a manner that recognizes the equality of our fellow citizens? *Civilization* and *civil* sometimes don't go together, and civilization and civic virtue have grown farther and farther apart since Athenian times. Can we help inculcate this virtue in people? I suppose we can impose legal duties on them. In Australia, voting is mandatory: if you can't demonstrate a valid reason for failing to vote, you face a fine of $20; if the matter goes to court and you are found guilty, that amount can increase to $170 and you may even face criminal conviction. Not exercising your right as a citizen can criminalize you! As a result, the 2010 federal election in Australia had a 93.2 percent voter turnout. Compare that to 61 percent in Canada in 2011. Surely those numbers speak for themselves.

Some say family is the best place to learn how to behave towards each other as citizens. And it is true that in healthy, functional families there will be love and protection. The idea of encouraging life and protecting the vulnerable is something that can be applied to our public lives as well. But the concept of the family, particularly the nuclear family, is rather fraught with the difficulties of individual personalities and the intensity of family life, particularly now with delayed adolescence and blended families. I don't know that there is any evidence to prove that being brought up in a good family inculcates democratic virtues. Children seem to be the luck of the draw, the genes rather kaleidoscopic in their settling patterns. Nuclear families do not necessarily lead to the kind of responsive interactivity that citizenship requires. In Don DeLillo's

riveting novel *White Noise*, one of his surly char-
acters contends that "the family is the cradle of the
world's misinformation," protecting us by "sealing
off the world" and allowing "fictions [to] proliferate."
The family, with its emphasis on unity and identification among its members, can cultivate misan-
thropy, distrust, and disdain.

Starting in the eighties with the Thatcher and
Reagan administrations and their tax cuts, dereg-
ulation, and reduction of welfare, citizens were
expected to become models of initiative. According
to this philosophy, any help given to the poor created
and recreated dependency — citizens would follow
bureaucratic rules simply to collect their payments.
The ability to support yourself somehow became
an important part of citizenship. Citizens had to be
self-supporting, otherwise they couldn't be citizens.
They had to earn a living, and any social benefits had
to be cut back through "workfare" programs. While
initiative and entrepreneurship can be encouraged
by markets, markets do not give a sense of civic
responsibility, justice, or the common good. And
what are we to make of today's income disparities,
when Canada's top one hundred CEOs make on average 171 times the Canadian average wage of $46,634
a year? Another way of putting it is that just as the

average Canadian is wrapping up his lunch break at 1:11 p.m. on January 2, his income for the year has already been amassed by the top one hundred CEOs.

I think that in Canada, volunteerism is the ultimate expression of civic virtue. It is considered a public good, and to be a volunteer is to be a participant in the creation of that public good. This was understood by my predecessor, Governor General Roméo LeBlanc, who instigated the Caring Canadian Award, which I was privileged to give out across the country for six years. This award honours people known in their communities for spending time with others for the benefit of others. The astonishing result is the creation of civic decency and mutual help that have the intrinsic virtue of being personal, direct, and consistent. These awards are given to people who for decades have driven for Meals on Wheels, who fill out income tax returns for indigent people living in nursing homes, who sew doll dresses from scraps from the Salvation Army to make toys for underprivileged children. The variety of work done by volunteers in Canada is enormous, and it is quite rightly heralded.

What we don't know is how rare this is in the rest of the world. Arguably, Canada has the largest proportion of people engaged in volunteer activities of any population in the world. I recently told a French friend that during the Heart and Stroke campaign, a hundred thousand volunteers went door to door in February, our coldest month, canvassing for donations, and $10.5 million was raised in that one month. She was incredulous, because in France almost nobody volunteers; the citizenry expects the state to undertake these tasks and considers the government to be the guarantor of legitimacy and excellence. By contrast, in Canada we have brought volunteerism to a very fine resolution. Students in Ontario, for example, have to fulfill forty hours of volunteering in order to graduate from high school. In 2003, during a scorching heat wave in France, 14,802 mostly elderly people died from heat-related causes in their homes. No one thought to knock on doors to ask if anyone needed help. In 2013, roughly a million people in Toronto were without heat and electricity for up to a week in freezing weather. Nobody died as a result of the lack of heat and light. Neighbourly action and the care of police and fire departments assured this outcome.

It is important to note that people do not join volunteer organizations in order to prove that they are good citizens. Volunteers have motives that are altruistic, and these motives are valuable and must be acknowledged. Canadians seem to feel that volunteering makes them feel good about their lives. People want to have good lives, own houses, go shopping without worrying too much about overspending. And because we are all so much richer than we ever were, we don't understand that as a society, we in Canada were always a poor country and that, to a large extent, that poverty created our national character.

It has been said that no one is too rich to receive and no one is too poor to give. I have seen that old saying in action over the years. The urge to volunteer comes from recognizing a need and deciding that you, as an individual, can help fulfill that need. Our civic virtues are best exercised when we act selflessly in response to a need.

MARGARET THATCHER FAMOUSLY SAID: "There is no such thing as society." I have always begged to disagree with this statement since I first heard it from her, a politician whom I interviewed and personally found unappealing. Society is made up of many human beings, not all of whom are alike, want to be alike, or like each other. We cannot have a country, a province, a city, a neighbourhood without sharing with others. What is good is that we are, by structure, forced to come to terms with rules for living together, and that is what has created our societies. Sharing citizenship is a way of taking the good with the best. The Quran tells us that we were all created by a single Creator and therefore are all part of an original project. Mrs. Thatcher did not believe in society; she viewed individuals as grasping for pieces of a limited apple pie. To me, that is a simple view suited to simple minds. The world is much more complex, and the history of all civilizations tells us that to deny society is to deny the longing of human beings to be part of one another.

It is important for us to acknowledge what we owe to each other as citizens who belong to the entity called the state and participate in the creation of that state. There is an equilibrium, a balance, that makes it possible for us to tell the difference between our personal choices and those choices that are necessary in order to become functioning members of a larger entity that may not always express our specific beliefs, fondest dreams, and personal ambitions.

No country at any time answers all the needs of all its citizens: the way in which we can affect what our country does is to express ourselves through participation in all public activities and not simply in a final (however important) act such as voting. The important thing about our relationship to each other as citizens and to the nation is the social mobility made accessible through our interaction with others and through the freedom we enjoy in our democracy.

When other countries in the world today look at Canada and the way in which we have developed as an immigrant nation, they can hardly understand why and how it happened. Some Europeans have said to me that they think multiculturalism has worked in Canada because we have such a large country. It is as if our immigration and settlement policy was successful because we were able to distribute people evenly, say every 100 kilometres or so, over the vast surface of our geography. It is hard for people from other nations to understand that we do not treat people as outsiders because they are different from us; we have learned over the past forty years how to accept difference because we ourselves were different.

As such, we in Canada call immigrants who wish to become citizens "permanent residents"; in

the United States, which is so vaunted as the melting pot welcoming its "huddled masses yearning
to breathe free," immigrants are called "resident
aliens." That difference in terminology is highly
significant: in Canada residency comes first and
permanence will be transmuted into citizenship.
Our citizenship process moves from acceptance
to inclusion. Eighty-four percent of immigrants in
Canada become citizens; in the United States only
40 percent decide that they will become citizens.

Within the five or six years that newcomers usually have to wait to become full-fledged citizens in
Canada, they learn how to assess what their life
will be like if they decide to commit permanently
to this country. This period of engagement seems
to be particularly fruitful; it has been to our benefit and will continue to be — as of 2030 Canada's
net population growth will be entirely attributable
to immigration. This will make it possible for us
to continue to nurture the kind of society we have
established, with its medical benefits, public education, cultural activities, and of course infrastructure like roads. If we do not have a steady increase
in our population, we won't have the public mon-
ies necessary to support all these public institutions
and services. We need our immigrants and new

citizens to become part of our country in order for us to maintain the country as we know it and love it. And we will change and adapt as we receive people from different parts of the world. At any average citizenship ceremony in your town today, there will be about fifty new citizens who come from an average of twenty-eight different countries. No other country can talk of its growth in population in these terms. We are unique.

Until 2000 it was all but impossible to obtain German citizenship without evidence of German descent. The primitive tom-toms linking blood to nationality are very slow to lose their resonance. When I look around me in the south of France at the Provençal people and the various Algerians, Moroccans, and Tunisians who now live there, it is very hard to distinguish them from each other. Mediterranean people around the shores of that great sea have been raiding the area and breeding together for thousands of years; to talk of distinctions associated with blood makes no sense in today's world. It is only in costume, spirituality, and language that differences appear.

Between 1991 and 2001, the number of mixed unions in Canada increased by 35 percent and is still on the rise today, noticeably in those with university educations. So as Canadians have greater access to higher education, we can expect to see greater numbers of mixed unions. I take these figures as a very hopeful sign that if the long-form census is ever reconstituted, in fifty years a majority of people will list their racial background as "Canadian."

THERE IS A WONDERFUL exchange in one of my favourite novels of all time, Ernest Hemingway's *The Sun Also Rises*, in which Lady Brett Ashley's boyfriend drunkenly misbehaves, and she whines to her would-be suitor, Jake, that he behaved "damned badly" but "he had a chance to behave so well." Jake replies, "Everybody behaves badly. Give them the proper chance."

The point of having a civilized society focused on equality and on the common good is to create a structure in which people do not have the chance to behave badly. In Canada, we have been slowly learning how to give people the chance to behave well.

Years ago, a colleague told me how tired she was of people asking her when she had emigrated to Canada from the United States. She was a descendant of Black Loyalists, and her family had been in Nova Scotia since the late eighteenth century. The Black inhabitants of Nova Scotia have been systematically ignored, and their role in our history has not only been downplayed but frequently eradicated. Only in the past fifteen years have we come to realize that the history of these people, who are our fellow Canadians, has been systematically destroyed or ignored.

Between 1964 and 1967, the destruction of Africville, the Black community in Halifax, passed without the tremendous indignation that it should have aroused. I remember news reports at the time showing that the whole community was going to be taken away from their homes and rehoused, and that their settlement would be bulldozed for other purposes. There wasn't a huge outcry, as there would be now, some decades later. At the time, the words *Black* and *poverty* were inextricably linked, and somehow we were made to feel that it was a good thing that Africville was going to be replaced by something else, something better, something whiter.

In 2001, when I first went to Shelburne County in Nova Scotia, and in particular Birchtown, I saw maps showing the Black Loyalists' original homes

in what would later become the United States. I
was also shown the freedom papers of the Blacks
who had accompanied Loyalists to Canada after
1780 and thereby gained their freedom because
they were on the "right" side of the Revolutionary
War. I continued to be disturbed by the fact that as
Canadians we had written their story right out of
our collective history.

Growing up, I knew that the Underground
Railroad had helped the nineteenth-century abo-
litionists by bringing escaped slaves to Canada. I
had also spent some time in the area around Owen
Sound, Ontario, where Black people had settled;
some of the geographic names, such as Negro Creek
Road, reflected this history. Among European
settlers in Canada, the status of United Empire
Loyalists had always been very high. Somehow,
Black Loyalists were not afforded that status. Yet
some three thousand Blacks came to Nova Scotia.
Some came as slaves with the white people who
owned them. And some came free, because they
had served in battle for the British.

In 1770, before the American Revolution, there
were already seven free Blacks in Annapolis Royal.
Between 1776 and 1782, thousands of slaves came
with their white masters, mostly from Boston,

Charleston, and Savannah. What is most interesting is that very few of them were plantation workers. Most had talents as bakers, blacksmiths, and carpenters. And apart from the terrible shock of the climate, they were able to take their part in the pioneer society because of those skills. Even though they gained freedom, they did not gain freedom without misery. Land was given out to all Loyalists, but the Black Loyalists were given the least desirable land — they were at the end of the receiving line. Poorer land, less access in every possible way. In Birchtown, you can visit a reconstruction of a pit house, a primitive dwelling that amounted to a hole dug in the ground covered with boughs to shelter it. This is where Black immigrants would have spent a winter, two winters, in conditions that basically defy all description. Yet these new citizens persevered because they wanted to contribute to society and have a chance at a new life. They were willing to overcome failure, to suffer through delays in acquiring land. And what carried them through this harsh existence? Basically, their religious faith and their belief that a Divine Providence would keep them going. The promise of freedom was the greatest promise of all.

Ten percent of the new immigrant population

to this area was Black, but that did not mean that society opened up to them. The sad fact is that discrimination and bigotry went on for much too long. I remember talking during my visit to a man whose family came to Birchtown with the Loyalists in the eighteenth century. He told me that after having served four and a half years overseas in Canada's Armed Forces during the Second World War, he came home with his brother, who had also served our nation's army. They sat down in a restaurant in Halifax, wearing civilian clothes for the first time in nearly five years, and were refused service.

There are societies that have this kind of history — a history of discrimination and racism — and have not really evolved. We have such a shameful past, but I think on the whole we have changed, or tried to change, as a society. In looking at Black history in our country now, we know that the Black Loyalists are taking their place in Canadian society. George Elliott Clarke, who won the Governor General's Literary Award for Poetry, wrote a poem describing how Blacks have helped build our country from its very earliest foundations in Nova Scotia. And if they were not able to take their place right away as the baker or the shopkeeper, it wasn't because they couldn't do the work; it was because they weren't allowed to. Now those barriers have gone, and we hear George Elliott Clarke in "Guysborough Road Church":

we are the black loyalists;
we think of the bleak fundamentalism
of a ragged scarf of light
twined and twisted and torn
in a briar patch of pines.
and then, of steel-wool water,
scouring the dull rocks of bonny
bonny nova scotia —
this chaste, hard granite
coastline inviolate;
[. . .]
we are the world-poor.
we are the fatherless.
we are the coloured Christians
of the african united baptist association

The acknowledgement of Black Canadians and their history as Loyalists was hard-won and took two hundred years. But now the past is accepted as history, the present as full citizenship.

WE CANNOT BELONG TO a country unless we know it. As an immigrant nation, we were poor. We came to a land that was rich in natural resources and had been occupied for millennia by Aboriginal peoples who knew and understood the land and how to live with it and in it. We, as settlers, came and destroyed that bond of human beings and nature. We are still trying to recover from that wound.

Our culture is founded on three pillars: Aboriginal, Anglophone, and Francophone. It has made the idea of a melting pot impossible for us. Perhaps we are more comparable to a tray of melting ice cubes than a mosaic, as the literary critic Malcolm Ross noted. As we melt together we keep our shape. We have always been able to accept and open ourselves to others. And we've always had one of the most cosmopolitan cities in the world — Montreal, where French and English were spoken and where there seemed to be a willingness to let people be themselves. When I was growing up, Montreal was the de facto capital of Canada; I grew up wanting to live there. I thought it had a great role to play in the imagining of a new, more diverse and open society. Montreal was the tryout town for the first Black ever admitted to organized baseball. Montreal had an openness that its writers, like Hugh MacLennan, celebrated. At the time, I think Toronto envied and then emulated Montreal's cosmopolitan nature.

In writing about Canada as an immigrant nation, Malcolm Ross described it as "the impossible sum of our traditions." I agree with his theory that since the beginning of the seventeenth century, living in this northern part of the northern hemisphere, we have been able to accommodate our historical baggage — baggage that comes from somewhere else — by infusing our way of life with different kinds of influences. From this we grow. Ross points out that "the ghosts that walk our Canadian lanes crowd in on us from every nook of place and time. Our sense of time becomes multidimensional. Our sense of place, enlarged first by our own largeness, by the endless hopeless horizon of our land, shatters all horizons."

No one coming from elsewhere can reproduce their home country in Canada. Most of them don't want to. That is why they left. And that is why they have come to our country, because it already exists in its constitutional and historical entirety. They don't have to create it. Most of us who were already here when they arrived didn't have to create it either. We came and Canada accepted us with its tradition of parliamentary democracy, the common and civil law, bilingualism, public health care, and public education.

But how we go about living with each other in the decades to come is the challenge that everyone — immigrants, new citizens, established citizens, and native people — will have to meet. For most immigrants (and I am speaking out of personal experience and out of an ability to decipher and often decode what others who have shared similar experiences to mine feel), the stance that we have is the stance of deliverance. We who have come here very recently will surprise everyone. That is what makes Canada one of the most exciting countries to live in. The surprise element of our society keeps us vibrating with energy, curiosity, and a constant need for balance or equilibrium. We are walking a tightrope of our own expectations.

We are showing by our living together how those who have not belonged can belong. Because we know that immigrants cannot remain *they*. They will be, and are becoming, *us*. Just as *we* became *you*. And that *us* learns French and English because we know the complexity of the world, and we know that learning another language or two can't hurt. We know that participating in politics is a way of gaining a voice after the muteness of being uprooted from one's society and having to learn another language, and being therefore transplanted. And we know that physical well-being is part of the egalitarian expectation.

I came to this country as a refugee. I didn't willingly choose this destination. But once it became our destination, my family and I determined that it would be fully ours. And I don't think I'm alone in this. I see that will, that desire, that commitment shining out of the eyes of Roma schoolchildren singing in a choir at Queen Victoria Public School in Toronto's Parkdale neighbourhood. I see it in the backward glance of the Somali taxi driver who asks me how long I've been in this country. I see it in the swift, competent movements of the beautiful Korean owner of my local coffee bar, who serves the best espresso in the neighbourhood. I found that I could embrace the history of Canada (although when I was in school, it tended to be the history of Great Britain, but Canada came into it in the end, after the White Cliffs of Dover). I knew that I could understand this land, its ancestors, pioneers, and Aboriginal peoples, even though my direct forebears did not have any notion of such people or such events.

It was through imagining that I could be part of

it that I did become a part of it. My Grade 7 teacher, Miss Bernice Jackson, who came from Arnprior, Ontario, and had a wooden leg, said to me: "You weren't born here, but everything you do and will do will prove that you know what it is like to have been born here." I took that as my endorsement to belong, and I have never, ever felt any differently. Everybody, like me, who makes the conscious choice that this is going to be their home and native land becomes implicated in all of our history, and therefore implicated in the consciousness of our past. In her resonant fiction, Mavis Gallant explored the Canadian psyche like no other, perhaps because she lived most of her adult life in France, where she adopted a perceptive detachment about what we used to be like in the forties and fifties. You can never read Mavis Gallant without understanding something about the development of who we are as Canadians. Describing in a short story a character who represents the old WASP makeup of Canada, she wrote: "Flowering in us was the dark bloom of the Old Country — the mistrust of pity, the contempt for weakness, the fear of the open heart."

It is very important that we know where we have come from emotionally as a nation in order to understand how we are now evolving. *Mistrust, contempt, fear* — that is the old language. We who have come here have brought with us a new vocabulary of trust, respect, and confidence. If we learn to speak this new language by imagining the Other and by being part of an evolving whole, we know that we are all in this together. That we can make our belonging to this country as citizens real. That we can show our citizenship in the world as a different kind of citizenship — our citizenship of rights, responsibilities, and a common language of esteem, confidence, and perception.

Twenty-five hundred years ago, Pericles said to the Athenians:

> We live under a form of government... called a democracy. Its administration is in the hands, not of the few, but of many... We are open in our public life. We are free from suspicion of one another in the pursuits of everyday life. We feel no resentment if our neighbour does as he likes. We obey... laws which bring help to the oppressed and those which bring upon the wrongdoer a disgrace which all men recognize. We throw our State open to all the world and we never... [prevent] anyone from seeing or

burning anything... We are ready to meet dangers depending on the courage which springs from our manner of life rather than the compulsion of laws.

That exhortation is a direct call to our courage, to recognize and act on the possibilities beyond our private life and goals. This kind of courage depends on our understanding of the public good and on the acknowledgement that we all can participate in the creation of a society that benefits each and every one of us. Perhaps this is what we have been trying to create in Canada, even if we have not said it to ourselves in words. We are a society of difference. We are disparate. We are diverse. We come from all over the place — morally, intellectually, spiritually, geographically, and physically. But we must understand each other's realities. In doing so we will be able to recognize that others are not like us and never will be, but we still have to give them their space, as they, we hope, will give us ours.

I think many of us share a dream of Canada, a country of the imagination that we hope and work for. We dream it into being. All of us are fortunate to have been welcomed into the circle of dreams of our Aboriginal peoples. And I believe that most immigrants — because most immigrants that I knew or identified with came from loss — helped to dream their own children into being. The diversity of our country lies not in the difference between urban and rural, settled and wild, but in the peculiarities of a country with the sum of its traditions stunning us into silence.

CHAPTER FOUR

UBUNTU

PICTURE A LARGE SOCCER stadium filled with a
hundred thousand people. They have come from a
hundred nations for the state memorial service of
Nelson Mandela, known affectionately as Madiba
by his fellow South Africans. Rain pours down as
though the skies also mourn this great man's death,
but the crowd waves its umbrellas in excitement.
The staircases are thronged with people in yellow,
orange, and green. They are here for HIM. They are
here to honour arguably the greatest human being
to have lived in the past hundred years — a beacon
of courage, an icon of suffering, a paragon of forgiveness. Brought up to be a chief of the Thembu
nation, Mandela used his skills as a lawyer to defy
apartheid and spent twenty-seven years in prison,

emerging to lead his country by humble wisdom and generous example.

I belong to a generation of students of the fifties and sixties who were radicalized personally by South Africa. Although South African wine was cheap, we vowed never to drink it; although Rothmans cigarettes were filter-tipped and glamorous, we pledged never to smoke them; although Outspan oranges were delicious, we promised never to buy them. By boycotting products from South Africa, we felt we could help cripple the regime economically or, at the very least, make the government realize that we did not condone apartheid, which had become its official policy. When I think of how human beings treat each other, I always think of South Africa, because it was the first deep awareness I had that we all belonged to each other, that it is wrong for a state to deny humanity on the basis of race. Apartheid is the antithesis of belonging, and it defined for me what we must never accept, what we must help wipe out. Rarely in my life has the difference between right and wrong been so clear.

The Canadian delegation at the memorial service included five former Prime Ministers, two former Governors General, and several other political figures. Standing in the rain, I remembered how Canada's relationship with South Africa had played out in 1961. Having become a republic, South Africa had to reapply formally for membership in the Commonwealth, as India had done after its independence in 1947. Members from the Caribbean and African countries, as well as India, saw this as an opportunity to exclude South Africa because of its abhorrent official racist policy. The "white" member nations — Australia, New Zealand, Great Britain — wished to accept South Africa again. Prime Minister John Diefenbaker had discussions with the persuasive Prime Minister Nehru of India and found himself in a quandary. The Canadian Prime Minister was a booster of all things royal, all things British, all things Anglo-Saxon. Was he going to go against Britain, Australia, and New Zealand, and join countries like India, Jamaica, and Barbados that were opposed to readmitting South Africa?

Canadian students doing graduate work in Oxford, Cambridge, and London signed a petition against the readmittance and delivered it as a group to Mr. Diefenbaker in London. Robert Bryce, then Clerk of the Privy Council, was asked by Mr. Diefenbaker what he thought the Canadian people would think. In his memoirs, Bryce says he told the Prime Minister the Canadian people would approve of excluding South Africa because of its racist policy. As a result, Canada aligned with India and the other "non-white" nations. A declaration was made that racial equality be a requirement for Commonwealth membership. With that, South Africa withdrew its request to rejoin.

We showed that we were willing to confront our white relatives and do the right thing. We demonstrated that we wanted a colour-blind Commonwealth. As a result, a lot of young people like me voted for Diefenbaker in the 1962 election. Young conservatives like the future Prime Ministers Joe Clark and Brian Mulroney were galvanized by Canada's position, and held true to it with an anti-apartheid stance that brought great honour to Canada. In 1986, Prime Minister Mulroney called the South African policy "reprehensible and repugnant" and imposed tough sanctions against the promotion of tourism and new investment there. It was this important Canadian action that helped to end apartheid.

One day after Mandela was released from his twenty-seven years in prison, he called Mulroney to thank him for Canada's actions against the apartheid regime. Mandela continued to recognize

Canada's leadership amongst the Commonwealth nations; he made a point of maintaining his relationship with Mulroney, and when he came to Canada when I was Governor General, he spoke with warmth and intensity about the important role our country and its government had played in ending apartheid.

During apartheid, I went to South Africa and spent several weeks there preparing a one-hour documentary for the CBC. The atmosphere was tense and eerie; locally hired members of our crew were informants; I was officially classified as "white" because the evil absurdity of the regime decided that I was. Nelson Mandela had been in prison for thirteen years on Robben Island, and most observers, including me, felt he would die or be killed there. We did not realize then what we know now: this man, who was born an African prince and became a lawyer, was committed to fighting the injustice being done to all Black people and would learn to fight brutal inhumanity with courageous equanimity, insane racism with quiet reason, and unjust violence with forgiving civility. And the whole world reverberated for twenty-five years with the graceful elegance of his forgiveness.

After nearly thirty years, Mandela emerged

from prison. He was able to look at everyone, no matter what their colour, no matter what they felt about him, and engage their spirits, capture their hearts. Like his compatriot the Nobel Peace Prize winner Desmond Tutu, he embodies the African concept of Ubuntu, mankind's first social thought.

UBUNTU IS AN ETHICAL value that originated with the Bantu peoples and has been upheld by African societies for millennia. It is a statement of family cohesion and coherence that accommodates all living things. The concept of Ubuntu emphasizes our connectedness with each other in the past, the present, and the future. The concept tracks back through tribal Africa to prehistoric times. Several million years ago, in the Great Rift Valley, one of our earliest ancestors sat by a fire, shaping humanity's first tool, a hand axe. These exquisite objects are the first utterance of a new emergent consciousness: dig, cut, scrape, chop, pierce, hammer — actions that speak of social organization, extended families living and working together to secure their survival. I am what I am because of what others have been in the past, and what I am now in the present will be a part of me in the future.

This sense of connectedness, this symbiosis of all humanity, is the very essence of what we can be for each other and how we belong to each other.

Ubuntu implies seeing another human being as yourself and treating them as you would treat yourself, with love and respect. The Zulu proverb *"Umuntu ngumuntu ngabantu"* means "A person is a person because of other persons." This means that any failure to act in a human way is a failure of Ubuntu, and therefore someone who lacks Ubuntu is not really a human being. Each of us is a human being because of other human beings: we depend on each other for our well-being. It then follows that if we depend on others to be human, we are bonded with them. It is only through others that we gain our ability to attain our full humanity.

No organized religion, political ideology, or philosophical school can lay claim to Ubuntu. The Christian concept of *agape*, which is Greek for "love," is the closest idea from the Western tradition. Agape is the evocation of the love of God for his creation ("God is love," 1 John 4, verse 8), and later it was broadly used to denote charity — love in an all-encompassing sense ("If I speak with the tongues of men and angels, and have not charity, I am as a tinkling cymbal," 1 Corinthians 13, verse

1). The Christian doctrine of love teaches that God loves us, His creation, and therefore we are imbued with His love and are urged to love others who are created equally by Him. This is the act of grace, which is a spiritual expression of the idea of belonging. The emphasis here is on the individual reaching out to others, as opposed to the identification of the self coexisting among other selves, which is the concept behind Ubuntu. Nevertheless, the idea of agape and the kindness of love promotes the vitality and necessity of stepping outside one's self. It therefore follows that the cult of individualism which is so prevalent today can lead only to the most profound and severe personal isolation. If the individual is the only guide and centre for all meaning, then society makes no sense.

SOME SCHOLARS WHO STUDY the concept of Ubuntu — colonial scholars, needless to say — consider the philosophy to be primitive, childlike, and leading to a culture of dependency. The idea of the interdependence of all human beings is wilfully misinterpreted in order to denigrate the idea that we are mutually dependent. Where does individualism fit into this worldview? these scholars ask.

Doesn't the individual fear for her own personality if her essence as a human being depends on other human beings? Where is the triumph of the self, the triumph of ego? Some have attacked the concept of Ubuntu as standing in the way of social and economic progress, creating generations of people devoid of personal ambition or responsibility. Stephen Theron, for one, has described Ubuntu as "simply sidestepping the slow Western development of the idea of personal responsibility, charted in the Bible and elsewhere...Without this consciousness" he continues, "the fruits of technology cannot be enjoyed...The concept of Ubuntu teaches Africans to evade responsibility and hide behind the collective decision of the tribe."

The opposite of Ubuntu, then, is a particular kind of blinkered self-interest. According to this doctrine, an individual's well-being and security trump the needs of the group. One accumulates more while others make do with less, and all social and economic disequilibria are attributable to the Darwinian imperative that has shaped the ascent of man since we trudged out of that Great Rift Valley in Africa. Nature isn't fair. Nature isn't nice. Look at global warming. Those who believe in Ubuntu claim that it is our collective responsibility to take

care of the earth. But those who believe in the triumph of the individual have their own way of interpreting the data. Climate change, as catastrophic
as it may be for certain groups globally, presents
astonishing new economic opportunities here at
home. Once the Arctic is ice-free, new trade routes
will open up and our own Northwest Passage will
be violated forever in order to accelerate global production; those who want it so much will move in
and drill for even more oil and gas, because global
warming has opened the door to the final frontier
of fossil fuels.

The pull of Western economic philosophy has
been strong. Political philosophers such as Thomas
Hobbes, David Hume, and Adam Smith are read
(and often misread) to justify selfishness and
reinforce the idea that only self-interest and greed
motivate the individual. We have lived so long with
the Cartesian idea of "I think, therefore I am" that
it has all but blinded us to the concept of what it is
to be a person in all human manifestations. There
is something so lonely and almost sad about thinking and being with the emphasis on the "I." And it
puts a terrific amount of pressure on our individual lives, wants, abilities, dreams.

This emphasis on rationality undermines

continually our understanding of Ubuntu. We are told in the New Testament to love one another as we are loved by God, and we are told in the Quran that we are one because we have been created by a single Creator. Neither of these religions, to pick just two that are alive here in Canada, tells us that the individual is the most important thing in the world. On the one hand, we are told to love one another as we are loved, which implies a bond of energy and need; and on the other hand, we are told that we are part of each other because one single force created us and fused us together. This means that our personhood is derived from other people, is nourished by other people, and grows with other people.

In our New Gilded Age, the quiet voice of Ubuntu has been drowned out in the polarizing din of right-versus-left politics. Communal relationships and institutions that work for the common good and represent the shared values of civil society have fallen out of fashion. But none of us can ever be totally independent and self-sufficient. The responsibility and duty we owe to each other is universal. We learn very early in life that we need not only to accept help but also to give help when it is needed.

In some ways, we in Canada have actually lived the Ubuntu philosophy, because our early concept of community comes from the Aboriginal people, upon whom we depended to learn techniques for survival when we first came to this land. In the world vision of Aboriginal peoples, there is no separation of the individual from the group. The Other is always present, and the Other is not necessarily another human being but often a manifestation of the natural world — an animal, a fish, a tree. When the Aboriginal people on the west coast say they are the people of the salmon, they don't mean simply that they fish salmon. They *are* the salmon. Totem poles depict these integrated representations — the eagle, the bear, the fish — piled one on top of the other. And this is integration of the most meaningful kind: I am as I am because of the way we all are together. I owe my existence to others. What is sufficient for the group is sufficient for me.

It was only with the arrival of European settlers that the idea of the accumulation of wealth took root in Canada. Early Europeans who went to Africa were amazed to have found a people who didn't believe in gathering up wealth. In 1926, on the west coast of Canada, the RCMP broke up the last potlatch held by the Kwakiutl people. A potlatch is a feast in which a chief gives away huge amounts of goods to show his benevolence. By the early twentieth century, these goods included sacks of flour, umbrellas, and bolts of cloth. This tradition flew in the face of the established European order: the accumulation of goods for oneself, one's own family, one's own people; it horrified the posture of self-aggrandizing personal consumption.

The idea of sharing is much older than the concept of accumulating goods. We all share life, and we all participate in the same energy field, the same fundamental substance. The essence of our common humanity allows us to recognize in each other our similarities rather than to differentiate ourselves by pulling away from the Other. When we can be part of the Other, we agree fundamentally that we are all evolving at the same pace, that all humans are equal on the evolutionary scale. It is stated in the Quran that the Creator could have made us all the same but He did not, because the challenge of being different meant that we would have to learn how to get along with each other. The only way we can do that is through the recognition of our common humanity. As Roméo Dallaire said, "We are all human beings and no human being is more human than any other."

But difference must be encouraged. When the French philosopher Voltaire went into exile in England in 1753, he wrote that there were many different religious sects — not just Catholics and Protestants. And he observed: "If there were only one religion in England, there would be danger of despotism. If there were only two, they would cut each other's throats. But there are thirty, and they live in peace and happiness." Little did Voltaire know that he was really describing the Canada of today.

IN 2010, THE CHANCELLOR of Germany, Angela Merkel, declared multiculturalism dead. This in a country where multicultural policy included educating the children of Turkish guest workers in separate Turkish schools so that when they were sent home they would not have lost their language.

Compare this to a country like Canada, where 2,500 citizenship ceremonies are conducted across the country every year. Each one welcomes between thirty-five and fifty people from an average of twenty-eight different countries. And a recent survey found that 89 percent of Canadians believe that someone born outside the country can become a good citizen. Ninety-five percent of respondents said that the primary criterion for a good citizen is the belief that men and women should be treated equally. Eighty-nine percent felt that in order to be a good citizen you also have to follow Canada's laws. Eighty-two percent agreed that you have to accept others who are different. Eighty-two percent thought citizens should vote, while 80 percent said that you had to protect the environment. Sixty-five percent of respondents said that you must respect other religions. Sixty-two percent said that you must know something about Canada's history. Strangely enough, 27 percent of people who were born in the country said freedom and democracy were a necessity for citizens, while 29 percent of landed immigrants said the same thing. Only 5 percent cited quality of life as the thing that made them proud to be Canadian and, just slightly higher, at 6 percent, was being respected by other countries.

The survey is fascinating because it reflects a gender-equal, law-abiding, tolerant, voting, and ecology-minded population. But the challenge will always be to maintain our diversity, to accept and to recognize each other as part of the same family. One way in which we have failed at difference in our society is the way we have treated, and continue to treat, our Aboriginal people. The First Nations and Inuit are among the three founding peoples of this country, along with the Francophones and the Anglophones. Georges Erasmus, the former National Chief of the Assembly of First Nations who led the Royal Commission on Aboriginal Peoples (1991–1996), said:

> The ideals of a good life [are] embedded in Aboriginal languages and traditional teaching. The Anishinabek seek the spiritual gift of *pimatziwin* — long life and wellbeing, which enable a person to gain wisdom. The Crees of the northern prairies value *miyowicehtowin* — having good relations. The Iroquois Great Law sets out rules for maintaining peace, *Skennen kowa*, between peoples, going beyond resolving conflicts to actively caring for each other's welfare. Aboriginal peoples across Canada speak of their relationship with the natural world and the responsibility of human beings to maintain balance in the natural order. Rituals in which we give something back in return for the gifts that we receive from Mother Earth reinforce that sense of responsibility...Most Canadians subscribe to these same goals: long life, health and wisdom for self and family; a harmonious and

cohesive society; peace between peoples of different origins and territories; and a sustainable relationship with the natural environment.

It is painful to hear these words, because we have to acknowledge that we have not met those goals. As early settlers, we came upon the First Nations and the Inuit and sought to make the ownership of property the great divide between them and us: "We own this" became the rallying cry over "We share this."

I felt a personal responsibility when, as the representative of the Crown, I re-enacted treaty ceremonies, including one that was held at Lower Fort Garry in Winnipeg in 2001. At such ceremonies, reverence would always be paid to me as the embodiment of the Crown. When I performed these functions, Aboriginal people of all ages always addressed me as "Grandmother."

That treaty ceremony re-enacted in 2001 ended with the statement that the bond "will hold as long as the sun shines, the rivers flow, the grass grows." The native peoples entered into the treaties with good faith, and I would like us, whose ancestors signed those treaties, to honour them. Despite the fact that over the past four hundred years, millions of immigrants have arrived on these shores and helped build this country, we will not be able to continue to negotiate difference in our country until we have honestly fulfilled our promise to our Aboriginal people. The evidence of our betrayal is all around us — on the reserves, in the cities, in diabetes, in fetal alcohol syndrome, in suicide. The history of our nation is made up of a complex network of accords and agreements — the Quebec Act of 1774, the Constitution Act of 1867, and all the treaties with the native peoples across the country. But we have not lived up to our end of the bargain: with our own First Nations, we Canadians have failed in our Ubuntu project.

CITIZENSHIP IS MORE THAN patriotism with privileges. And it has to be balanced against the competing and compelling pull of individualism, which assumes that all individuals are independent of each other and that relationships can be abandoned when the cost-benefit ratio no longer works, in which case all relationships can be impermanent, manipulative, or apathetic. Citizenship also requires imaginative intuition that the situation of your neighbour could be your situation in the future. Or, in our immigrant society, that a newcomer's arrival to our country with one suit-case was your arrival in the past. As someone who came to this country with one suitcase, I have never lost the sense that I came from that minimal place where everything had been taken away. It is part of my recognition that I am human and that I belong to every experience that human beings undergo. The playwright Terence, who had been brought to Rome as a slave from Carthage in the second cen-tury BC, stated it succinctly: "I am human; noth-ing human is alien to me."

If a society is healthy, it will be able to look at what everybody believes, and it will cause those within the society to look at their own beliefs and see what foundations they have for, say, their Christianity, their Judaism, their Buddhism, or their atheism. To be able to observe others in your system and to question your own beliefs is inher-ently healthy. The worse thing that can happen is to reject other people's belief systems because they are not your own. This is the very basis and foun-dation of exclusion, because it seeks to destroy that connectedness, that community, that Ubuntu.

The concept of acceptance incorporates both understanding and tolerance. It is very important to point out that this does not mean that people set out to be good to each other; rather it means that the context of the human being is always the community. So now I'd like to promote what I will call "passive acceptance." Most people don't like the word *passive*, because it implies impotence, weakness, or indifference. To me, passivity is not exactly the opposite of action. The passivity I am talking about is mixed with awareness and a latent curiosity. In passive acceptance, there has to be watchfulness and there has to be the desire to contextualize ourselves with other human beings around us. Often we must let things happen and simply observe.

The evocation of emotion to resolve the issues that arise in a complex society is not useful in a diverse society. Love will not iron out the differences between us. Certainly I would never question that we need love as individuals. But to talk about love as the sole means for unity misleads and deludes us about what gives us our strength as a unique society. The problem with love is that it does not leave room for differentiation, and the mind and the heart will sometimes go in different directions. Just loving people is not something you can ask of a state. Nor do many nations set out to be loveable. Many of them have had great success by being unlikeable, and often loathsome.

Our society must be based on a different set of tensions that includes emotion but emphasizes analysis, acceptance, and curiosity. We cannot create a civil society by including only the people we like and with whom we share similar interests and goals. That is called friendship. And a society, a country, is more than a friendship.

The English philosopher and political scientist Michael Oakeshott observed:

> Friends are not concerned with what might be made of one another, but only with the enjoyment of one another; and the condition of this enjoyment is a ready acceptance of what is and the absence of any desire to change or to improve. A friend is not somebody one trusts to behave in a certain manner, who supplies certain wants, who has certain useful abilities, who possesses certain merely agreeable qualities, or who holds certain acceptable opinions; he is somebody who engages the imagination, who excites contemplation, who provokes interest, sympathy, delight and loyalty simply on account of the relationship entered into.

Oakeshott goes on to say that one friend cannot replace another. The relationship of friend to friend is dramatic, not utilitarian; the tie is one of familiarity, not usefulness. Friendship is a relationship sought and relished for its own sake and enjoyed for what it is, not for what you can get out of it.

Much as friendship is a remarkable and necessary thing for individuals, we cannot base or build a society around it. Affectionate feelings will not cure all ills. And just because somebody is not your friend does not imply that they are your enemy. The ground between is where we have to operate as a decent society.

As I conceive of it, Ubuntu is about the fundamental necessity of human relationship and acceptance of the Other. It is not an emotional relationship. Countries cannot be built on emotional relationships. The scale is simply too large.

OUR SOCIETY HAS TO continue to be created through the syncretic tensions inherent in our differences. Our true strength will come in building a good society not only with those whom we like, admire, and share values with, but also with those whom we do not like and whose values and inherent beliefs are different from our own. It is with these people, as well as with those we respect, love, and emulate, that we have to create our society. The only way to accept what we do not like is to understand that it is part of the greater consciousness, part of a deeper understanding that we are related because we are human; that we belong to the world, just as those we dislike do; and that they play their part just as we must play ours. We must look upon ourselves as fortunate because, as the Quran states, our challenge is to learn to cope with these differences in order to build a better society.

The society we built here in Canada — the society we *are* building here — didn't just happen; it required vigilance, planning, and constant effort. And it still does. Our national anthem in French says, "*O Canada! Terre de nos aïeux*" — "Canada, the land of our ancestors." Although we are all different, we also come from roots, and roots have to be rooted somewhere. Our roots come together in the common desire to have a country. In this country, where almost everybody came from somewhere else, we have become our own ancestors. Everybody is our ancestor. That is how we have lived. The past, the present, and the future are part of our own identities, our own being, our own time.

Even though many languages are now spoken in this country, we have not built a Tower of Babel. We who came after the Aboriginal people brought saints and heroes, and we honour them here even though they were never "over here." The poet D. G. Jones believed that Canada is

> less a question of nationalism than of an imaginative stance towards the world, towards nature and culture, past and present, the life of the body and the life of the mind, the fact of death. It's a question of finding a satisfying interpretation of these fundamental elements in human life so that one can take a stand, act with definitive conviction, have an identity.

I think the creation of a diverse, healthy society is ultimately a kind of religious quest. When the element of grace enters our active imagination, it is possible for us to change, to transmute, and to identify.

So we must not live under the delusion that we can love other people into a democratic state. A society is about managing to live together with the maximum amount of liberty within a structure that provides enough security that we can exercise our responsibilities.

People do not care only about themselves. All evidence points to the fact that most people in moments of acute crisis do not behave out of individual selfishness but out of a sense of their connection to others. We always wish to be part of something, and when we are part of that thing, our behaviour shows that we know we depend on each other. Perhaps out of pure evolutionary selfishness, our initial instinct is to reach out and help another human being.

For more than six years, I had the unique experience of giving out Bravery Awards to Canadians. The first time I really understood what this award meant, I was faced by twelve men, all of whom were wearing a simple dark blue uniform. The citation read that they had rescued people from a highway in Saskatchewan after a tanker truck ignited and was burning so intensely that the tarmac rolled up and melted. I assumed that they were all members of the volunteer fire department. But no, I was wrong: these men had been taking a break in a coffee shop at a rest stop along the highway. A few were farmers, two of them were mechanics, others had office jobs. Some of them were volunteer firefighters but in different communities. Somebody came running in and said, "A truck is burning up on the highway," and all these men rushed out to help rescue the driver, to alert other drivers, to risk their lives.

Another man saw a truck ahead of him burst into flames and swerve onto the shoulder, shuddering to a stop. The man stopped, broke a window, and dragged the driver to safety minutes before the vehicle exploded. There were several incidents in which people witnessed someone attempting suicide off a bridge into a large body of water and leapt into the frigid water to save that person's life. In many cases, those who had done the saving had never again been in contact with those whom they had saved. The life was worth saving; the action was done; the meaning was there in the act.

I had always somehow assumed that people risked their lives to save their family, their neighbours, their friends. But awarding these medals over the course of six years made me aware that people will help total strangers, endangering their own lives in the process. I remember speaking to the man who broke the window of the flaming truck to get the driver out. I asked him what was going through his mind when he did this. He answered, "I looked down at that guy, and I thought, that guy is *me.*" No words could express Ubuntu more clearly: this was the total imagining of the Other.

THERE IS AN INTERSECTION I frequently drive through that links the eastern part of Toronto with the western part. It is a four-way stop, with one road going through one of Toronto's most beautiful ravines, the Don Valley, and the other connecting commercial Bloor Street with the leafy confines of the Rosedale neighbourhood. The road that cuts through the ravine ultimately leads to a highway called the Don Valley Parkway, so it is a serious commuter artery.

Whether it's rush hour or one o'clock on a quiet Sunday afternoon, every driver stops his car at this intersection and waits to take his turn, proceeding in counter-clockwise fashion. To me, this is so quintessentially Canadian that I want to bring people from all over the world to this intersection to witness it. In France, two drivers would charge towards each other, rolling down their windows and raising their fists. Perhaps only in the Scandinavian countries could I imagine a similar scenario taking place.

To me this intersection represents the kind of Ubuntu we have in Canada. First and foremost, it shows self-restraint and the exercise of personal responsibility. What I find particularly moving is the capacity to wait for the other driver, to be patient if he doesn't go ahead when it's his turn, and instead to make eye contact across the intersection to engage him and let him know it is his turn. In the years that I have driven through this intersection, I have never seen a collision.

These citizens are acting with public awareness within the context of basically healthy institutions. This sense of purpose and this awareness that other people occupy the same space keep our institutions — like Parliament, like the law — running smoothly. As the German philosopher Jürgen Habermas noted, "The institutions of constitutional freedom are only worth as much as a population makes of them." That intersection would not work if we did not have civic awareness, if each citizen did not bring the values from his private life into this public sphere. It represents a citizen meeting his responsibility towards others with equal measures of restraint and permission.

Cooperation is another value that springs from this kind of spontaneous action. But the cooperation is utilitarian: it is in the citizen's self-interest to negotiate this intersection with efficiency and with no waste of emotional capital in order to get to where he was headed before he had to stop. He is also responsible not only for his own vehicle but tacitly for the other three vehicles at that intersection. He has taken care not to damage the others, nor to hurt himself. This is Ubuntu as an organizing principle. It is in this realm of cooperation and consideration that modern citizens show virtue, or *arete*, as the Greeks call it. And it is this virtue that enables us to live together, to stay whole, and to renew.

CHAPTER FIVE

GROSS NATIONAL HAPPINESS

TODAY IT IS CUSTOMARY to go to a fine concert hall with wonderful acoustics and listen to a ninety-person choir and an orchestra perform J. S. Bach's Mass in B Minor. This is one of the most sublime musical works ever written, and it is certainly worthy of being heard more than 250 years after Bach composed it. It is not an exaggeration to use the word *sublime* to describe this music. The words of the Mass, beginning with the Kyrie Eleison, then moving to the Gloria and through to the ending of the Agnus Dei, are written specifically for the rituals of the Mass of the Christian Church. For Christians, the exquisite harmony of the music, the blending of the soloist and the choir, the sound of the woodwinds and the strings are all part of a

service of worship of God. The fact that this compo-
sition is now performed in concert halls, as opposed
to churches, does not mean that it is without spiritual meaning. But it does show that this piece of
music can be appreciated aesthetically by people
to whom the idea of God may be anathema, and
for whom the idea of a Messiah offering deliverance from the wages of sin is a fairy tale. Today, it
seems that religious symbols have meaning only
when they are reflected back in the mirror of secularism. But true secularism means the acceptance
of many beliefs, not the eradication of them all.

Religious music like Bach's Mass in B Minor is
appreciated in a world that, to put it mildly, does
not appreciate God. Belonging to a religious faith
is a kind of paradox in the twenty-first century.
I am not the first person to note that as society
has grown further away from organized religion,
Baroque music, oratorios, and operas dealing with
religious subjects have become more and more
popular. I would argue that when you listen to a
piece of music that has deep religious meaning, it
is not stripped of that meaning simply because you
might not personally believe in God. The music
itself is imbued with faith, with belief, and with the
accretion of centuries of listeners whose lives are

elevated from the ordinary to the extraordinary by hearing it. In this way, a whole society, both spiritual and secular, has acknowledged aesthetically that we are part of one civilization.

The Canadian literary critic Northrop Frye said, "We participate in society by means of our imagination or the quality of our social vision. Our vision of what society is, what it could be, what it should be are all structures of metaphor because the metaphor is the unit of all imagination. Logical thinking in this field seldom does more than rationalize these metaphorical visions." What Frye is telling us is that we participate in each other's imagination even if we are not consciously aware of doing so. We are a part of each other's wishes, hopes, and, yes, dreams.

IN EXAMINING HOW CITIZENS must relate to each other in the world today, I want to explore some of the ideas of the late-nineteenth-century German philosopher Hans Vaihinger, which reflect what Frye said. A follower of Kant, Vaihinger represented abstractions by using fiction, which he argued is a useful way to bridge our models for living with the realities that confront us in our cities, our countries, our societies. His philosophy of As If can be boiled down to this: you act As If something is true if the result of that act of imagination will bring benefits. If you accept someone's word As If it is true, you will bring truth to that interchange, even if you are lied to. It is better to be lied to than to lie, and better to be wronged than to do wrong. This is an ethical no-brainer. So when we imagine newcomers into being as citizens, we treat them as though they have a right to vote; as a result, the act of imagining leads to the reality: soon they will become capable of voting.

Vaihinger relied greatly on another German, the nineteenth-century philosopher Friedrich Carl Forberg, who exhorted his readers to

Believe that virtue in the end will triumph! ... Believe that no good action done or merely designed by you, no matter how small and obscure and humble it be, will be lost in the haphazard course of things! Believe that somewhere in this course of things there is a plan, imperceptible to you, it is true, but calculated on the ultimate triumph of the Good! ... It is true that in all this you cannot scientifically demonstrate that it must be so. Enough that your heart bids you act *as if* it were so, and merely by so acting you will prove that it is so.... [The good man] feels compelled by his conscience to do all that he can to help towards the attainment of the this end... He accordingly believes that the end he sets before himself, the supremacy of the Good, is an attainable end... As a matter of *speculation*, he may leave on one side the question whether this end is possible or impossible; but when he *acts* he must behave *as if* he had decided in favour of its possibility, and he must endeavour gradually to draw nearer to that end.... It is not a duty to believe there exists a moral world-government... our duty is simply to act *as if* we believed it.

Even if we are attempting as citizens to create an order in which we can all live an appropriate life, in which we have moral regard for each other and value each other's abilities, we still might think it likely that circumstances could arise which, according to Vaihinger, would render our ideal impossible. Forberg's response is:

Unquestionably that is so, if success be the final aim of effort, the goal the final aim of the runner.

But what if the striving were a final aim in itself!
What if there were no goal to be attained or, what
is the same thing for the runner, only a goal set
at an infinite distance? What if the goal were
there for the sake of the race, not the race for the
sake of the goal?

The point is that a good man does good even if
he does not believe in a moral world order; he acts
As If he does believe in it. Perhaps we should not
be thinking about whether we can chip the edges
off ourselves so that we can form a tiled pattern,
as though we were planning to cover some inter-
nal floor. Perhaps we are not meant to have a goal
that can integrate, accommodate, justify all of our
lives. But we can learn something very useful here
about the way we interact with each other. We are
too easily discouraged when other people disap-
point us: we feel it means that our society is failing, that our goals are unattainable, that we have
not taken the right road towards a better life for all
people. The philosophy of As If encourages imaginative creation. If consensual coalescence around
responsibilities, rights, and obligations cannot be
met, then we must make a great leap of the imagination into the realm of possibility. And it is in that

realm of hope that citizenship can come to have its true value.

The world of culture, the world of the mind, and the examination of the spiritual are all parts of that central movement defined by As If. When we behave As If we care about each other, As If we encourage everyone to be part of the group, As If we are all equal, we are actually living a metaphor.

This place of the imagination is lacking in today's world. In global terms, *citizenship* refers primarily to the movements of people and the integration of foreign elements. By contrast, here in Canada we have been able to recreate ourselves instinctively, behaving As If this pluralistic society, as we know it now, has always existed. Some critics say that we are living in a "convenient fiction." But operating on the principle of As If has led to the creation of the Canadian citizen. We behave As If newcomers can take their place, go to school, learn our two official languages. Because we have lived As If, our multicultural, diverse country has become a reality. Other phrases describe this philosophy — "taking it on faith," for example — but As If goes one step further because it acknowledges that when we live As If, the As If can become the actual reality. As If has a wishful, desiring quality about it, and there is nothing wrong with that, especially if behaviour follows. Then we can justify the fictions we live by.

In essence, we are all writing the narratives of our own lives; we all wish for things, work for them, and find out if they are viable. The tyranny of the factual is not a necessity for living a rich human life. I loved it when author Farley Mowat said that his truth was not bound by facts. Facts are noticed and catalogued by even the most unimaginative observer; truth goes beyond the facts and reaches the essence of what facts only illustrate. It doesn't really matter whether or not Mowat ate mice, as he depicted himself doing in *Never Cry Wolf*. He was able to convey to us what it was like to eat mice and what it meant to him. Anybody can eat a mouse, but not many people can make us feel what it is like.

Years ago, I had occasion to interview Dame Edith Evans, one of the greatest actresses of the twentieth century. Celebrated for her work on the stage, she was particularly famous for playing Millamant, the brilliant and alluring heroine of William Congreve's Restoration comedy *The Way of the World*. Evans was an astonishing-looking woman when you stared into her eyes but someone you could pass in the street without noticing. Indeed, when I interviewed her, she looked unremarkable. There was nothing particularly out-standing about her physical appearance — her hair, her eyes, her mouth. I could not help but ask her how she felt about playing a beautiful woman. She looked at me sharply and then, with a good deal of amusement, said: "You mean, because I'm not beau-tiful when I'm sitting here talking to you." I said: "Yes, that's what I mean." She smiled brilliantly and responded: "I'm not beautiful sitting here talking with you, but when I get on the stage I can be the most beautiful woman in the world." Evans was not simply playing the part of an actress who is part magician and has learned the tricks of moving seductively, twirling her costume, and tossing her head. I believe her underlying message revealed an important truth about how one lives one's life: it isn't simply a matter of the presentation; it's a mat-ter of being able to inform and change and work in a manner that surprises and delights.

Our Aboriginal peoples know this transforma-tion; in their society, the As If changes a person's sex or even their entire form from a human being to a salmon or a wolf. We could live transforma-tive lives if only we activated our imaginations and took the journey.

It is interesting to think of the philosophy of

As If as a necessary fiction of human thought. The assumption of truth in the face of false ideas makes a better life possible. Since the truth is unknowable, and maybe not even graspable, we can at least work with this healthy fiction to create a healthy society. It is interesting to note that the American arch-cynic H. L. Mencken hated the philosophy of As If. He stated scornfully that "very few fictions remain in use in anatomy, or in plumbing and gas fitting; they may have even begun to disappear from economics and [this philosopher's] work is not a system of philosophy in any true sense; it is simply a footnote to all existing systems.... It is curious, but it is unimportant." In our creation of Canadian society we have shown that the philosophy of As If is not merely a curiosity, that it is important, and that it can be lived.

IN TODAY'S PLURALISTIC, DIVERSE, and in some cases highly polarized societies, how does a nation determine and agree upon its communal As If? Let me offer one example of a country I visited and came to admire greatly.

In 2003, I travelled to Bhutan, one of the most beautiful and unique countries in the world and different from so much of Asia. The Kingdom of Bhutan lies to the north of India and shares borders with Nepal and Tibet. The Himalayas are at its northern border. With a population of roughly 750,000 people, it has one of the lowest population densities in the world, at nineteen people per square kilometre. (It is interesting to note that in roughly thirty years the population density has doubled!)

I remember walking along a path surrounded on both sides by hemp plants that came nearly to my shoulders. The landscape was filled with treed hillsides, and the green of the vegetation was astounding. The architecture of the towns and villages is traditional, so it's impossible to tell whether a building is two hundred years old or was constructed in the past year. The whitewashing, the tiles, the fresco paintings on the exterior walls are maintained, repainted, and refreshed, giving you the feeling that you exist in a place that has no time. Because of the nature of the landscape, the climate ranges from the subtropical to high alpine, and this mixture of hot and cold makes it unique.

A group of us had just walked several kilometres from a game reserve, where we were taken to see the Bhutanese national animal, the takin, which resembles Eeyore in *Winnie-the-Pooh*. This

goat-antelope is hairy, black, and about the size of
a large pig but with longer legs; it has an endearing
docile quality, probably because of its large snout.
We were walking through hills that led to the foot
of the Himalayas. But we were not preparing to
climb the Himalayas, at least not from the Bhutanese side of the mountains.

Years ago, the Bhutanese decided that they
would not allow people to climb those storied
peaks. Farmers said that when people attempted
to climb the mountains, bad weather would follow, and subsequently bad crops. So the country
decided to ban international climbing on their side
of the Himalayas. The Bhutanese have been very
careful about their contact with the world. They
demand that tourists spend a certain amount of
money per day in their country — in 2003 it was
US$350 per person per day — in order to create a
tariff wall around their society. In this way, they
have protected their culture and society from the
kind of tourism that has seen neighbouring Nepal
descend into a cheap haven for a good smoke.

We turned a corner and climbed a little hill,
where we rested at the top to gaze down at a group
of people gesticulating and releasing joyful, somewhat musical shouts. As we moved closer, we saw

a group of ten or twelve men wearing what looked like beautifully draped kimonos that came down to the knees, and white boots stitched with coloured patterns up the front and down the back. A tight belt was wound around the waist, with the top bloused over it. The patterns reminded me of Scottish tartans, the way the stripes and colours blended and yet stood out against the landscape. Each of the men carried a bow; some raised their bows exultantly over their heads with two hands. Further down the field was a large target. Archery is the national sport of Bhutan. The men were wearing the traditional clothing called *gho*, which the Bhutanese continue to wear to this day. The women among the group were wearing what's called a *kira*, a long dress made of beautifully woven thick silk. The fabric was fastened at the shoulders and worn under two small jackets of softer silk. There wasn't a blue jean or a T-shirt in sight.

We happened to be out walking on the day that is celebrated as the national birthday — not the birthday of the nation, but every Bhutanese citizen's birthday, which is celebrated on January 1. Many archery competitions are held to mark the festivities. The two teams stand at opposite ends of a long field, and when an arrow hits the target, the teammates hold hands and dance around the target very slowly, singing jubilantly about the sporting and sexual prowess of the successful archer, who is given a bright scarf that he wears on his belt. The national birthday makes for one big, happy party, fitting for a country whose goal for the measurement of progress is gross national happiness.

The Bhutanese idea of gross national happiness is based on the all-important Buddhist concept of interdependence. Buddhism teaches us that we are all interdependent; what we do affects those around us. We have to see ourselves as part of a larger system of cause and result. We cannot abstract ourselves from others, because we are interrelated with all things in these causal relationships. And, most importantly, we live in the same world as animals and the environment, and we have to develop a compassionate heart that focuses on them as well.

The Bhutanese are practising Buddhists, and monks are held in the greatest esteem. Their form of Buddhism, Drukpa Kagyu, is a school of Mahayana Buddhism. It is similar to Tibetan Buddhism, but it has its own unique set of beliefs and practices. Monks play a very active part in community life, and one son from every family usually enters an order at about the age of ten. The enormous and beautiful white monasteries, called *dzongs*, look like fortresses and are one of the most outstanding features of the landscape. They are a marvel of construction in wood and plaster and rise up the equivalent of eight or nine storeys by way of small, ladder-like stairs. A police officer is stationed at the entrance of every *dzong* to ensure that the Bhutanese are wearing proper clothing, the men in their *gho* and the women in their *kira*, and that foreigners are not wearing T-shirts, sandals, or shorts. Bhutan has a stable monarchy, steadily rising development, and increasing prosperity through the sale of hydroelectricity to India, all within the context of Buddhist belief and tradition. Its goal of gross national happiness is a deeply intriguing concept in today's world.

Four practices underlie the Bhutanese fundamentals for gross national happiness: generosity; ethics; patience, or tolerance; and perseverance. In 1972, Bhutan's fourth Dragon King, Jigme Singye Wangchuck, coined the term during a time when the country was adapting to modernization through its economy while still maintaining its unique culture and Buddhist spiritual values.

There is no question that when people hear about the Bhutanese concept of gross national happiness, they think it is some kind of romantic utopian idea, a childlike concept of the world. In the Western tradition, by contrast, it is generally assumed that the better off you are materially, the happier you are. But, increasingly, research shows that rising income levels do not correspond with rising levels of happiness. Of course, the Bhutanese would tell us that Buddha discovered this 2,500 years ago.

While Buddha didn't entirely reject the idea of possessing wealth (he recognized that a certain degree of material well-being is essential to living a happy life), what he did stress was that the ethical and moral life would bring genuine happiness. More importantly, Buddha rejected greed and the accumulation of wealth because they caused enslavement to materialism and the pursuit of wealth as an ultimate goal. Gordon Gekko's "greed is good" motto has no place in the Buddhist context.

So there are two kinds of happiness: one is anchored in a certain physical comfort and pleasure, and the other is inner contentment and peace. Aristotle's concept of happiness, *eudaimonia*, tells us that virtuous activity constitutes happiness. He said that "happiness is a certain activity of soul in accord with complete virtue." And although Aristotle says elsewhere in his writing that we can "call no man happy while he yet lives," his concept of happiness is not entirely contradictory to the Bhutanese idea. The Bhutanese look at the total context of collective well-being rather than emphasizing an individual's state as conditioned by material needs. Like Ubuntu, the Bhutanese ideal acknowledges that people must help each other in order to promote a healthy environment.

Nothing can be added to happiness to increase its value; happiness includes everything that has intrinsic value, and is therefore self-sufficient. And self-sufficiency doesn't imply solitude — intimate personal relationships, artistic creation, scientific discovery, and religious experience have value because they illuminate the mysterious in our lives and give depth and meaning to our actions towards others. This happiness is active because it empha- sizes "living well and acting well." Action, as Han- nah Arendt said, is never possible in isolation. It requires both a subject and an object. To be isolated is to be deprived of the ability to act. There is also an element of stability — true happiness cannot be extinguished by one incident or a sudden reversal of fortune. And it must also be available to any- one willing to strive for it. Action depends on the constant presence of other people, and as a result it's the exclusive prerogative of human beings. Whether we sing in a choir or play tennis or join a political party to support a candidate we believe in, we are inserting ourselves into the interplay of other people's lives.

IT IS AN INTERESTING exercise to measure the Bhutanese principles of gross national happiness in our society. First, let's look at *generosity*. As citizens, Canadians have a long history of practising generosity. We were, for most of my life, a country that cared for the world. Through institutions like the Canadian International Development Agency (CIDA), we gave aid in areas such as education, health, and agriculture. My fellow university students went abroad with the World University Service and Canadian University Service Overseas. It was considered normal to go to Rwanda or the newly independent Tanzania and work to establish a new university there. Georges-Henri Lévesque, the Canadian Dominican priest who started the university in Rwanda, was a Commissioner selected by Vincent Massey as a Commissioner for the 1951 Royal Commission on National Development in the Arts, Letters and Sciences, commonly known as the Massey Commission. The resulting Massey Report led to the founding of the National Library of Canada and the Canada Council for the Arts, a system of grants to institutions and individuals to "foster and promote the study of and enjoyment of and the production of works in the arts." The federal government established funding for the Canada Council in 1957 with the death duties from the estates of two rich industrialists, Sir James Dunn and Izaak Walton Killam. The linking of our cultural expression and our desire to help developing nations used to be typical of the way in which we saw ourselves and our role in the world.

We are also generous with each other when we volunteer, give to the United Way, or take part in any community activities. In volunteering to go to two World Wars on behalf of people we had never seen and knew almost nothing about, we performed truly selfless actions. Laying down your life for another life is in and of itself a virtuous act. That is what many of our young Canadians did when they served during those World Wars.

I remember celebrating the sixtieth anniversary of D-Day and the liberation of Holland with our veterans. It was remarkable to see how much the veterans enjoyed going back to the sites. Some wept as they walked the ground upon which they had lost their fellow soldiers, but not a single one suggested that those deaths had been in vain. They felt they had done something good for others, out of a spirit of knowing what it is to help, what it is to rescue, what it is to give. They participated in a collective activity based on the belief that they were liberating others from evil, that they were individually capable of giving themselves to protect and help others. They came from the sea in small landing craft and were attacked by an entrenched enemy on the shore. But they took the beach and began the liberation of a Europe that had been occupied for five years.

We learned this generosity from the way in which the native peoples welcomed us to this land: they taught us how to use canoes to navigate the rivers that took us to the heart of the continent, which we then claimed as ours. They showed us how to live in the wilderness and how to survive the cold. In return, we bartered for wealth in the form of beaver pelts, and with this first set of negotiations brought into being a trade that hugely benefitted us. The cooperation that we knew then was not pure exploitation; the Aboriginal peoples wanted to participate in the trade economy and we were able to oblige. We now acknowledge that our country was founded upon this reciprocity and we still live by it today, even though many have forgotten where this innate sense of cooperation in our national makeup comes from.

Of course, our climate has also been a formative force on our national character. Our climate *is* our character. You cannot live in a country with four distinct seasons — ranging from freezing winters to brutally hot summers — without acknowledging a need for cooperation. Whether it's in Manitoba or Ontario, after every major snowstorm there is always a front-page story about a farmer trudging through a kilometre of snow to invite people stranded in their cars to come to his home to warm up and spend the night. When we read these stories, we recognize ourselves. We behave with instinctive generosity, particularly in crises. Our cooperation is not a simple transaction of "I will give you this if you will give me that." Generosity is our stance; it is not about an immediate payoff. For me, generosity is the highest form of reciprocity. "Regular" reciprocity was essential to early Canada — we had to cooperate or die — and we still live by this value, even if we've long forgotten why. We Canadians cooperate. Generosity doesn't demand the quid pro quo of reciprocity.

For some years now, there's been a phenomenon known as "pay it forward" in coffee shops. Someone in line will pay for the next customer's coffee, and that person, in turn, will pay for the next person behind them. Eventually, of course, the chain is broken; someone doesn't pay it forward, and the chain of generosity ends. But the fun is in seeing how long it takes before the chain breaks. A few years back, a record was set in a Tim Hortons franchise in Winnipeg. Over the course of three hours, on a freezing morning just before Christmas, 228 people in the drive-through line paid for the order of the next customer. "An avalanche of kindness," one person called it. Two hundred and twenty-eight random acts of generosity in a row.

Collectively we are more than we are individually. It is in this idea of the collective that we exercise the second tenet of gross national happiness: *ethics*.

Ethical consideration — the way in which we behave towards each other — which I have pointed out is not based on love, friendship, or mutual interest, must order our behaviour. In this way, we can behave decently towards someone whose values we do not share, whom we don't like, whom we really don't want to share a meal with. We must accord the same consideration for her public space, her expressed opinions, as we would to our colleague at work or the people in our church group. We also should expect the same sort of treatment towards ourselves. Ethical behaviour means courtesy, sharing, and honesty.

The parable of the loaves and fishes in the Christian New Testament illustrates that everyone in the multitudes that day listening to the Sermon on the Mount, whether or not they believed what Christ was saying, shared equally when the fish and loaves miraculously became enough to feed everyone. In *The Life of Brian*, Monty Python's religious satire, some of the onlookers interpret the words so that they hear "Blessed are the cheese makers" and "The Greeks shall inherit the earth." It is a hilarious misinterpretation, but I also find it profound and rather moving. Even those who misinterpret, who do not understand, who cannot hear, or who garble meaning are included in the bounty. Ethical behaviour is the action that each of us must show in order to belong and to extend that belonging to everyone else.

Honour is not a fashionable concept today. In the past, people lived and died for their honour. And their honour was based on the perception they had of themselves in their behaviour towards others. Until recently, cabinet ministers resigned if a member of their staff had done something wrong: as the person in charge, they felt responsible for everything that happened under their watch. That is the concept of honour in public life, which used to be in our parliamentary tradition. It was accepted as part of the responsibility of being entrusted with public office. An ethical stance is not a narrow question of probity or of not lying or of not cheating. It is a concept of fair conduct and acceptable behaviour in a posture of openness and trust. And it involves interaction with the Other. Ethics is the scale upon which we balance our relationships with other human beings.

To act ethically is to act outside of any expectation of reciprocity. We act ethically because we believe in a higher set of values that goes beyond law or duty. Ethical action is an expression of our deepest understanding of our humanity. It is ethics that most clearly drives our attitudes and actions in the world beyond our fellow human beings: how we act towards our natural environment and animal life, the respect for all that we don't understand, our attitude towards the entirety of our human action. For example, in Canada we don't have a better

banking system because we have better regulations. We have better regulations because, I think,
we in Canada think in a different way. Regulations
always spring from social norms, and the social
norm in Canada is to be equitable. We are a com-
munitarian people (think of our history of survival
through snow and ice), and the community is where
equity and ethics reside.

Ethics is not merely a set of abstract principles;
ethics requires action. And it encompasses the idea
of the collective over the individual. Having been
welcomed in the First Nations circle when the first
settlers arrived, poor and helpless, shaped our society so that community counts more than anything.
Only by being open and acting ethically could we
have built our society and overcome what Malcolm
Ross described as the "impossible sum of our traditions," meaning that we have made the possible out
of the impossible with this country. True action, as
I pointed out earlier, is only possible in the context
of others. We cannot act in isolation. Paradoxically,
in Canada, with our huge land mass and relatively
small population, we have come together in order
to act together.

The third tenet of gross national happiness
is *tolerance* or *patience*. We in Canada live with

diversity without anxiety. As a pioneer society we knew poverty, loss, and hardship. We struggled to make our way in a country that didn't offer us any gifts, except that of personal freedom and the ability to live in harmony with the land, as exemplified by the Aboriginal peoples. It is also clear that tolerance is important in a frontier society. In order to survive, we needed the gifts of the entire community.

I am enormously grateful for having lived this part of the twentieth and twenty-first centuries. I grew up in our capital city of Ottawa, where French Canadians were not allowed to speak French in workplaces that were dominated by English-speaking retailers; where Anglophone and Francophone Catholics fought each other not only on the football field but also in the alleys of Lower Town; where your friends said their parents would disown them if they ever married a Catholic. And yet individuals were kind to everyone. There was no official stance of racism, even though the Chinese Head Tax was still in force and at school we were made to do projects about "Indians" by constructing small teepees on pieces of beaverboard to show how they lived their lives. Never did it occur to anybody to tell us that only sixty kilometres away from the capital was the reserve of Maniwaki, where Algonquin live. I never met a single native person until I went to university. It was as though their culture had died.

The fact that within my lifetime we have made adjustments and changes to create a more open and equitable society is a source of great happiness to me. We have come through a terrible 150 years in our relationship with the Aboriginal people, but that I hope is changing as well. This is where our patience, and particularly their patience, has to be put into practice.

And so we are still in the fourth stage of gross national happiness, which is *perseverance*. Perseverance is the child of dialogue and the democratic process. We have inherited this trait perhaps from First Nations decision-making, which can look slow to outsiders but is actually about striving for an equitable solution about the project of the moment: what is best for all of us? Perseverance tells us to think about both today and tomorrow.

We have yet to organize fairly our relationship with the Aboriginal peoples. We should find some joy in this relationship, rather than perceiving it as a wretched duty. We must listen, we must act. We must look at past failure as another tiny step towards success, as an inspiration for courage, and as an opportunity to practise wise compassion.

Parts of our country, like Saskatchewan and Manitoba, have made the most practical accommodations, teaching primary schoolchildren that everyone is a treaty person and encouraging the learning of Aboriginal languages. For more than thirty-five years, the University of Manitoba's Access Program has graduated native teachers, social workers, and doctors by understanding that the needs of young people who have grown up on a reserve are social needs, requiring personal mentoring and perhaps greater flexibility in terms of the school year.

Imagine what it is like to be an eighteen-year-old woman from a remote reserve in Manitoba, perhaps five hundred kilometres from Winnipeg, with one small child. You would like to continue your studies and you have gotten some financial help, but how do you make your way to Winnipeg when you have never lived in a city before? How do you find child care? How do you live the life of a student, which has been conceived for young middle-class people who have the nurturing care of parents? The Access Program helps with these needs: degrees, including demanding ones like medicine, can be obtained over four or five years instead of three or four. This kind of program is necessary if we really want people to belong and participate in the kind of society we have built. We are not asking that they give up their values, but instead saying we understand the background of native people who want to make their way into mainstream Canadian life. This is the best way of helping people belong: to walk the path with them as they become part of ordinary middle-class life while retaining their own values and way of life. This kind of adaptation of the educational system attests to the value of standing in the other's place, seeing from the inside what their needs are, and helping them reach objective goals with practical resources and cultural comprehension.

We also must persevere in the preservation and enhancement of our natural environment. Every citizen must understand the special relationship we have with our land or there will be no sense of stewardship in the future. Many people who come to this country are from cities, but many others are from small towns and villages where they have known what it is like to live in the countryside. Still, there is a big difference between countryside and nature. Our resources are very precious: water, forests, mountains, oceans, and minerals — this is where perseverance must be exercised to fulfill the fourth tenet of our gross national happiness.

As we have learned to extend our comprehension and mutual need to Aboriginal people, we have increasingly become aware of how they have shown us the way to understand and become part of our environment. Fifty years ago, we were just beginning to listen to what they had been saying to us about the natural world, acknowledging that we do not own the earth but are keeping it in trust for our children and grandchildren. And listening to their wisdom has had an effect on our attitude towards clear-cutting forests and turning lakes into acid. We have begun to learn that the earth is organic and alive and sentient, and that we as human beings are part of that life. We take our place in it; we must not dominate it.

When I visited the Nisga'a people in northern B.C. in 2004, some time after they had successfully negotiated their treaty with the federal government — a struggle that had taken the better part of the lifetimes of two of their chiefs — we went out picking the huge white mushrooms known as *matsutake* that grow under the moss. Even though the mushrooms were a cash crop, fetching astronomical prices when exported to Japan, my companions cautioned me that we must pick only about two-thirds of what we found under those appealing bumps on the forest floor. The Nisga'a followed a policy of sustainability for their export industry, just as they had when they picked the mushrooms only for themselves.

We are not perfect, nor are we perfectible. However, we are trying, and in that effort we are moving in the right direction. We need to learn from people like the South Africans, who have had the bitter and trying experience of institutionalized racism, so that we too can reconcile our past and let the truth set us free. We have not resolved the residential school question with a government payout; our conscience should not be assuaged when forty First Nations reserves still have no schools for their children; when fourteen thousand Aboriginal children, on and off reserves, are in foster care; when there is a shortage of eighty-five thousand housing units on First Nations reserves; when on-reserve schools receive $3,000 to $4,000 less per child than other Canadian schools; and when one out of five Aboriginal communities has a drinking water advisory.

This kind of shameful inequality has to be

expiated. As a society, we have to forgive and be forgiven for the inequity of native people. Hannah Arendt tells us that the act of forgiving can never be predicted, that it comes in an unexpected way; she tells us forgiveness is the only reaction that does not merely react but "acts anew and unexpectedly, unconditioned by the act which provoked it and therefore freeing from its consequences both the one who forgives and the one who is forgiven." Vengeance or punishment does not put an end to the original wrongdoing or its consequences, because it re-enacts an original trespass; instead of putting an end to the process, everyone remains bound to it. Only forgiveness breaks the chain reaction.

Canada has always been a forgiving society; immigrants who come here are in effect forgiven their past and start life anew, in a different landscape, with a new language. This new identity, this new belonging, is the essence of forgiveness for the past, for remembered suffering, for necessary sacrifice. If we cannot redress wrongs such as those we have committed against the native people, we become a punishing society that lets wounds fester, and wrongs continue endlessly and prevent healing from taking place.

We belong to each other in this country. Our

history spans hundreds of years, and we are unique. We are very different today from what we were in the eighteenth century. We have grown together, been plaited together like the intricate branches of the benjamina tree. But we must not be complacent.

I HAVE MADE BELONGING the interest of my life. I was, and am, a child of diaspora. I am someone who, for a while, did not belong anywhere. And I will always be someone who understands the everlasting anguish of not belonging. We arrived in this country under the shield of the Red Cross, stateless, as refugees. Then Canada took us in.

It was in attending public school that I truly felt a sense of place in this country. Still today I believe that a public education is the single most valuable institution that our society provides to help people belong. If we are going to continue to accommodate newcomers into society, we must continue to have well-funded public education — education paid for by the state, free for all citizens. This has been key to our success ever since our humble beginnings. Without public education, we cannot have a cohesive society, a society with shared values. Without public education, we cannot continue to fulfill the public good — that is, the internationalization and the continuation of our key notions and values from one generation to the next. We can do all of this only in a democratic structure, where all children are treated as equal, regardless of income. That is how people really learn to belong. That is what public education does. We want people who will take their place in our society, but that means we must make sure there are no barriers to inclusion for people who come here.

In *Reconciling the Solitudes*, the philosopher Charles Taylor said: "A prolonged refusal of recognition between groups in a society can erode the common understanding of equal participation on which a functioning liberal democracy crucially depends." We have depended upon the knowledge of complexity to become the kind of country we are. In a pluralistic society, everybody wants to be recognized for who they are, not for what other people see them to be, often mistakenly. And this is crucial to an individual's, as well as to a nation's, sense of identity.

So belonging is essential to us in Canada. We select our immigrants with the idea that they will become citizens. Immigrants are future citizens, and we recognize them as citizens in the making.

As Aristotle said in *Physics*, "With respect to what is eternal, there is no difference between *being possible* and *being*." New citizens take on the same responsibilities as existing citizens: obeying laws, paying taxes, voting. And once a new citizen is adopted into the family of fellow citizens, he must accept the good with the bad, both past and present, in order to contribute to and help shape the future. Canada is the land of our ancestors, as it says in our national anthem, and we are each and every one of us adopted by those ancestors. Newcomers are not invited to this country to spend a few years working, only to depart like migrants. *Migrant* is a very ugly word, and it should have no place in the Canadian vocabulary. *Immigrant* is the Canadian word. And citizenship is central to our immigration policy.

I truly believe that you can find a place to belong as long as there is a negligible amount of force against you. I was lucky to come to this country, where we operate in an atmosphere of benevolent neglect: we are left alone to get on with our lives. This is where perseverance and generosity come in. Canadians are generous even when they don't know it. To me, this flexibility is the generosity that leads to gross national happiness, because it allows people to persevere through hard times and come out on the other side.

We who have had everything taken away from us once, and sometimes twice, know what it means to begin that struggle and to continue it all our lives. And we can never listen to those who say their communities are fixed, their values forever, their identities unchangeable. Canada now has more people who know what loss is and what starting over means than people who don't. The shock of the loss of country, possessions, and status is what has informed us as human beings.

And we have all been immigrants in the past; we share a collective subconscious in a way that no other country does. Many countries have shared a collective trauma. What we have here is a collection of diverse traumas. That is part of the impossible sum of our traditions as well. We all know that we came from somewhere else originally, and we carry that history within us. It is part of our organism. Whatever country we originally came from, we cannot help but know within us, even several generations along, what kind of pain, loss, injury we endured. But out of that we emerge not unblemished but rather with the knowledge that living in this country has enabled us to recognize that the past matters but that it cannot damage, destroy, or annihilate us. The true meaning of perseverance in our larger conception of happiness is that we are not simply washed clean and made new, but that we are able to absorb and overcome by helping to create at every moment, with every action, with every vote, with every public commitment new standards for living life together, as a society, as a country. We have all been immigrants in the past. What matters is whether you define your life by what you have been able to recreate out of the past or whether you define it by what you have lost. And like the unexamined life, the life defined by loss is not worth living.

As Grand Chief John Kelly said, "The circle... gets bigger and bigger. Canadians of all colours and religions are entering that circle. You might feel that you have roots somewhere else, but in reality, you are right here with us." The Ulyssean ideal is true: we are striving and seeking, and we will eventually find the necessary means of creation, the act of the imagination that will continue to shape our unique place as Canadians in the world.

The subtitle of this book is "the paradox of citizenship." What is the paradox of citizenship? It is that we are most fully human, most truly ourselves, most authentically individual, when we commit to the community. It is in the mirror of our community — the street, the neighbourhood, the town, the country — that we find our best selves. We've been on a long journey through some of the history of the idea of the citizen, and what a story it is. It evokes an idea of what it is to live together, and the sometimes meandering path that idea has taken as it finds its way to us, today, in Canada. Above all, this is a story about people: the bearers of ideas who dream about what might be possible, what might one day become a reality. Aspasia and Pericles, the nameless citizens of Eygalières, the unfortunate Martin Guerre, the Black Loyalists, the South African activists — this is their story, which is to say this is our story, because each and every one of us recognizes ourselves in their struggles and their ideals. The dream of the citizen is the dream of a better world, with all its frailty, confusion, ambiguity, and hope. It's our turn to add to the story, to imagine the future of the citizen into being.

NOTES

CHAPTER ONE: THE CIRCLE WIDENS

Colin Turnbull, *The Mountain People* (New York: Simon & Schuster, 1987).

There is still much controversy about Turnbull's study of the Ik. Although many sociological details were disputed, the main thesis was basically never questioned: that all standards of mutual comfort or caring could disappear if the tribe were threatened to the point of extinction. I leave us to draw our own conclusions.

For the theatrical adaptation, see Colin Turnbull, Colin Higgins, and Denis Cannan, *The Ik* (Woodstock, IL: Dramatic Publishing, 1985).

Grand Chief John Kelly, "We Are All in the Ojibway Circle" (testimony before the Royal Commission on the Northern Environment, 1977), in *From Ink Lake: Canadian Stories Selected by Michael Ondaatje*, edited by Michael Ondaatje, 579–91 (Toronto: Vintage Canada, 1995).

The account of Eygalières draws primarily on the work of local historian Maurice Pezet, who has written extensively about the history of Provence. For further reading, see Maurice Pezet, *Les Alpilles* (Paris: Horizons de France, 1955).

Henry James and Edith Wharton both knew this part of France well; each travelled there separately, and once together. They wrote charming essays about the landscape and customs. For James's account "A Little Tour in France," see Henry James and Richard Howard, *Collected Travel Writings* (New York: Library of America, 1993).

There is some dispute about the Ligurians being Gauls, but local historians now subscribe to the idea that they were indeed the same people. Read Caesar's *Gallic Wars* or the popular French series *The Adventures of Asterix* for more details. Personally, I love Vercingetorix and have gone twice to Alesia in Burgundy, where he was defeated by Caesar.

Arles is a Roman city with beautifully preserved ruins, including a coliseum capable of holding twenty thousand people. Today it is used mainly for bullfighting, a favourite spectacle of the Provençal people that attracts Spanish bullfighters; its season occurs around the Christian spring holidays of Ascension and Pentecost. The city also has the remains of a theatre and an impressive collection of Roman sarcophagi, because people had their bodies shipped down the Rhone to be buried in this favourite cemetery.

Arles is also where Vincent Van Gogh came in February of 1888 — a remarkably creative time in which he produced three hundred painting and drawings in a year and a half, some of which are his most famous: *Starry Night over the Rhone* and *The Yellow Room*. It was here that he cut off his ear and where the population circulated a petition, after which he was confined to the asylum at nearby Saint-Rémy-de-Provence. The famous irises still grow in the courtyard there.

At the time that Eygalières gained its freedom, the people were in the process of legally losing their language. The 1539 Ordinance of Villers-Cotterêts was an edict that called for the use of French in all legal acts and official legislation. This was a move to centralize all authority to the state, based in Paris; to effectively discontinue the use of Latin in official documents; and to destroy the use of all other languages in France, including Occitan, which is the language spoken by the Provençal in Eygalières. In the late nineteenth century the rise of the Provençal language became identified with a growing literary movement. Its major figure, Frédéric Mistral, was the leading promoter in a group that wrote in Provençal called the Félibrige. Mistral, who wrote in Provençal only, was awarded the Nobel Prize in Literature in 1904. He was given this recognition for the "true inspiration of his poetic production and... his significant work as a Provençal philologist." It is a wonderful coincidence that his name is also the name of the fierce wind that blows down the Rhone Valley and is a true physical presence in all of Provence.

In the Eygalières of today, Mass is celebrated in Provençal on the Tuesday after Easter at the Chapel of Saint-Sixte. The women dress in traditional clothing, and little brioches that have been blessed are distributed. You keep the brioche for a year and eat a crumb every time you feel an illness coming on — a sure thing against all infections.

Dante wrote the *Divina Commedia* in a language he called Italian, but at the time it was really a mixture of the dialect of Tuscany with some Latin and other regional dialects. It is said that he seriously considered using Provençal for his writing because it was already the established language of a great literature, including the songs of the troubadours and accounts of courtly love. However, he made the imaginative leap towards creating an Italian language. Through his high ambition and literary purpose he established Italian as a vibrant language, and Provençal was the loser.

Jean Moulin as a hero has inspired some very fine biographies, all of which are readable. He seems to inspire biographical respect, which is not always true of controversial heroic figures. Before joining the Free French in London, he had been the Prefect of Chartres, the youngest holder of that office in France. In June 1940, when the Germans occupied France, he was arrested by the Gestapo and tortured. As he was concerned that he might give in, he cut his own throat with a razor but was found and recovered. He escaped and made his way to London in 1941 to join de Gaulle and the Free French.

For a thrilling experience of the French art of oratory, I recommend André Malraux's speech when Moulin's ashes were transferred to the Pantheon, the resting place of France's great men, on December 19, 1964. That magnificent funeral oration ends with these words: *"Aujourd'hui, jeunesse, puisses-tu penser à cet homme comme tu aurais approché tes mains de sa pauvre face informe du dernier jour, de ses lèvres qui n'avaient pas parlé; ce jour-là, elle était le visage de la France."* [Today, young people of France, may you think of this man as you would have reached out your hands to his poor, unrecognizable face on that last day, to those lips that never let fall a word of betrayal: on that day, his was the face of France.]

The vagaries of agriculture policies in the European Union have meant that the apples that were enthusiastically planted forty years ago have now been torn up in favour of peaches, apricots, and, increasingly, olive groves.

Thomas Lewis, Fari Amini, and Richard Lannon, *A General Theory of Love* (New York: Random House, 2000).

The Frost quote comes from a letter to Louis Untermeyer penned in January 1916. See Robert Frost, *The Letters of Robert Frost to Louis Untermeyer* (New York: Holt, Rinehart and Winston, 1963), 22.

The problem with the penguins developing desire for their human keeper was that it prevented them from mating with their own kind. Reproduction is at an end if the object of desire not only doesn't desire back but also doesn't have equipment in the right place to respond.

For the original account attributing this experiment to Frederick II, see G. G. Coulton, *From St. Francis to Dante: Translations from the Chronicle of the Franciscan Salimbene, 1221–1288* (London: Nutt, 1907).

Natalie Zemon Davis, *The Return of Martin Guerre* (Cambridge, MA: Harvard University Press, 1983), 44, 81, 86, 89, 102–3.

The Martin Guerre story was subsequently adapted into an American film called *Sommersby*, with Richard Gere and Jodie Foster. The major dramatic flaw in that film was that it was perfectly obvious why Jodie Foster's character would welcome back Richard Gere's character as her husband! Davis is the outstanding scholar of the Middle Ages of our time. I have benefited enormously over the years from her writing and her energetic wisdom.

The idea of stolen identity is compelling. For instance, the story of Kaspar Hauser, the so-called Prince of Baden, captured the imaginations of Verlaine, Melville, and, most recently, Peter Handke and

Werner Herzog. In modern times the story of Anastasia, the supposed only survivor of Russia's Romanov dynasty, haunts people's imaginations. We are very attracted to stories of stolen or assumed identity because the need for us to find ourselves is so great, and often very tenuous.

Thomas Lewis, *The Lives of a Cell: Notes of a Biology Watcher* (New York: Viking Press, 1974), 14. When it was published, this book caused many of us to understand the interaction of culture and science in a completely new way.

For the story, see Mary McCarthy, "The Man in the Brooks Brothers Shirt," in *The Company She Keeps* (New York: Harcourt, Brace, 1942). McCarthy's ability to analyze and dissect the habits of women after the Second World War is remarkable. Her novel *The Group*, which appeared in 1963, had a major impact on me, second only to Betty Friedan's *The Feminine Mystique*.

CHAPTER TWO: THE GLORY THAT WAS GREECE

Gertrude Atherton and Franklin Horn, *The Immortal Marriage* (New York: Boni and Liveright, 1927).

Gertrude Atherton wrote fifty-two books and innumerable magazine and newspaper articles during her prolific career and was thought to be a minor-league Edith Wharton. Another book she wrote about Greece, called *The Jealous Gods*, featured Alcibiades, a less heroic figure than Pericles but fascinating; it's very readable still.

When I was a teenager, Aspasia was not my only example of female daring. The pugnacious feminist Charlotte Whitton became mayor of Ottawa — the first woman to be mayor of a major city in Canada. She dominated Ottawa politics over a period of two decades with her strength of character and her wit. She was famous for saying, "Whatever women do, they must do twice as well as men to be thought half as good. Luckily, this is not difficult." Controversy raged when it was suggested that her name be attached to a public building;

eventually a utility crane in the harbour of Ottawa's Britannia Yacht Club was given the honour.

At the same time I discovered Gertrude Atherton I also fell in love with opera through the Metropolitan Opera radio broadcasts. My first passion was *La Traviata*. Like Aspasia, as my mother pointed out, Violetta had her strong points but she was also a bad woman. Not, my mother added, what I would be, of course.

Atherton, *The Immortal Marriage*, 46.

Atherton, *The Immortal Marriage*, 50.

Thucydides, *The Landmark Thucydides: A Comprehensive Guide to the Peloponnesian War*, edited by Robert B. Strassler, translated by Richard Crawley (New York: Random House, 2008), 110–11: 2.37–38.

Atherton, *The Immortal Marriage*, 218–19.

F. Scott Fitzgerald, *The Crack-Up*, edited by Edmund Wilson (New York: New Directions, 1993), 306.

This account of democracy in the classical world, and in particular classical Athens, has drawn on a number of sources: Ryan K. Balot, *Greek Political Thought* (Toronto: Wiley, 2008); Kurt A. Raaflaub, "Contemporary Perceptions of Democracy in Fifth-Century Athens," *Classica et Mediaevalia* 40 (1989): 33–70, and "The Breakthrough of Demokratia in Mid-Fifth Century Athens," in *Origins of Democracy in Ancient Greece* (Berkeley: University of California Press, 2007), 105–54.

Aristotle, *The Politics*, translated by Carnes Lord (Chicago: University of Chicago Press, 1984), 183-84: 1317b11–13.

Thucydides, *History of the Peloponnesian War*, excerpted in Balot, *Greek Political Thought*, 59: 2.37.2–3.

I have a personal preference for Balot's translations of many of the Greek texts I have drawn on; I find them direct and colloquial, although nuances are perhaps rendered differently in other translations. Take, for instance, Crawley's translation: "The freedom which we enjoy in our government extends also to our ordinary life. There, far from exercising a jealous surveillance over each other, we do not feel called upon to be angry with our neighbor for doing what he likes, or even to indulge in those injurious looks which cannot fail to be offensive, although they inflict no positive penalty. But all this ease in our private relations does not make us lawless as citizens" (*Landmark Thucydides*, 112: 2.37.2–3).

Plato, *Republic*, from adapted translation in Balot, *Greek Political Thought*, based on the Grub-Reeve translation, 58: 557b–558c.

Thucydides, *History of the Peloponnesian War*, translated by Rex Warner (Baltimore, MD: Penguin, 1972), 158: 2.60.

For this distinction, see Isaiah Berlin's "Two Concepts of Liberty," in *Four Essays on Liberty* (Oxford: Oxford University Press, 1969).

Regarding the speech of Inuit at feasts, the rhythm of such conversations while food is being eaten reveals the very nature of the most comfortable and aware of human interactions. Speech is not a formal obligation but an inevitable ebb and flow between people. As Leonard Cohen sings, "It's just the way it changes, like the shoreline and the sea."

Herodotus, *The Landmark Herodotus: The Histories*, edited by Robert B. Strassler, translated by Andrea Purvis (New York: Random House, 2007), 398.

For me, the histories of Herodotus and Livy and Caesar's *Gallic Wars* are the three most thrilling documents of the history of the ancient world, because of the stories they tell.

Aristotle, *Politics*, excerpted in Balot, *Greek Political Thought*, 65: 1281a42–b7.

Atherton, *The Immortal Marriage*, 440.

Hannah Arendt, *The Human Condition* (Chicago: University of Chicago Press, 1998), 186, 176.

Arendt's writings in *The Origins of Totalitarianism* and *Eichmann in Jerusalem* oriented our political thinking in brilliant ways. The 2012 movie about her life by Margarethe von Trotta recounts her intellectual development and her relationship with Heidegger, Mary McCarthy, and *The New Yorker* magazine in provocative and revealing detail.

For a broader discussion of the place of democratic trust in Thucydides' account, see Balot, *Greek Political Thought*, 71–73.

Aristotle, *Politics* (trans. Barker, ed. Stalley), 231: 1317b16–17.

Thucydides, *Thucydides: The Peloponnesian War*, Book 2 (Cambridge: Cambridge University Press, 1989), quoted in Balot, *Greek Political Thought*, 82: 2.37.

I longed to learn Greek in high school, but it was not offered. After I became hooked on ancient Greece, I started to read Homer in Richmond Lattimore's translation during my year of Greek and Roman history in Grade 11, at Lisgar Collegiate with Ms. Meech. Thucydides was my favourite then for the sonorous phrases of his writing, and I still find it enormously soothing to read his passages on the Peloponnesian War. Ms. Meech regretfully but graciously docked me two marks on my final exam because I had not noted that the Battle of Salamis was a naval battle — and I have not forgotten it to this day. The best recent translation of Homer is by Robert Fagel, who is a poet himself.

Aristotle, *Politics* (trans. Barker, ed. Stalley), 117: 1283b.

For an account of Athenian metic status, as well as Aristotle's account of citizenship from "the outside," see Michael Walzer, *Spheres of Justice* (New York: Basic Books, 1983), 53–55.

For the classic account of the feudal order, see Marc Bloch, *Feudal Society*, translated by L. A. Manyon (London: Routledge & Kegan Paul, 1961).

From Burke's letter to Charles-Jean-François Depont, in *Edmund Burke: Further Reflections on the Revolution in France*, edited by Daniel E. Ritchie (Indianapolis: Liberty Fund, 1992), 7–8.

The French national anthem, "La Marseillaise," is the bloodiest that exists. It is the very fruit of the French Revolution and a memorial to its unforgiving violence:

Entendez-vous dans les campagnes	Do you hear in the fields
Mugir ces féroces soldats?	The howling of those fearsome soldiers?
Ils viennent jusque dans vos bras	To cut the throats of yours sons and consorts!
Égorger vos fils, vos compagnes!	They are coming into our midst
Aux armes, citoyens!	Take arms, citizens!
Formez vos bataillons	Form your battalions,
Marchons, marchons!	Let's march, let's march!
Qu'un sang impur	Lest impure blood
Abreuve nos sillons!	Water our furrows!

I heard this break out spontaneously, with explosive vigour, in a French bar when the French team lost to the Germans in the quarter-finals of the World Cup of soccer in the summer of 2014.

Edmund Burke, *Reflections on the Revolution in France*, edited by Frank M. Turner (New Haven, CT: Yale University Press, 2003), 31.

The kidnapping of Edmund Burke to right-wing causes remains a mystery to me. It is totally unjustified. John Stuart Mill's *On Liberty* and Burke's *Reflections on the Revolution in France* have had more influence on my personal political views than any others.

The English Revolution was successful because, although the king was beheaded, the English reformed their parliament and kept its history, their roots in the Magna Carta, and the common law. The French Revolution, because the Jacobins triumphed, destroyed everything in order to start anew. They got Napoleon as a result — really not a sensible or fruitful outcome.

Alexis de Tocqueville, *Democracy in America*, translated by Harvey C. Mansfield and Debra Winthrop (Chicago: University of Chicago Press, 2000).

Margaret Laurence, "My Final Hour," address to Trent Seminary, Mississauga, ON, March 29, 1983, reprinted as "My Final Hour," *Canadian Literature* 100 (Spring 1984): 197.

I first met Margaret Laurence and interviewed her before she became a novelist. She had written *The Prophet's Camel Bell*, which recounted sensitively and astutely the story of her life with her husband in British Somaliland. I subsequently read all her fiction with great joy.

CHAPTER THREE: THE COSMOPOLITAN ETHIC

Carl Jung, *Collected Works*, translated by R. F. C. Hull (Princeton, NJ: Bollingen, 1976), 17: para. 187.

Edmund Burke, "Speech to the Electors of Bristol," in *Select Works of Edmund Burke: A New Imprint of the Payne Edition*, foreword and biographical note by Francis Canavan, vol. 4, 12–13 (Indianapolis: Liberty Fund, 1999).

The Althing was located at one of the most spectacular geographical sights in the world, called the Thingvellir. It is also a place where the tectonic plates of Europe and North America coincide. This is enough to make you believe in pathetic fallacy. For further discussion of the Althing as an ancestor of our notion of parliamentary democracy, see Jesse Byock, "The Icelandic Althing: Dawn of Parliamentary Democracy," in *Heritage and Identity: Shaping the Nations of the North,* edited by J. M. Fladmark, 1–18 (Shaftesbury, UK: Donhead, 2002). The Icelanders still call their parliament the Althing, although it is now located in downtown Reykjavik. Their history has made a nation that is 100 percent literate. When the Marquess of Lorne was Governor General (1878–83), he visited recent immigrants to Canada from Iceland in their sod huts in Manitoba, and noted with great approval that every single household had books in it.

Aga Kahn, "Lecture by His Highness the Aga Khan: The LaFontaine-Baldwin Lecture (Toronto, Canada)," October 15, 2010, http://www.akdn.org/Content/1018.

Ten thousand Ismailis came to Canada in the early 1970s, mainly from the East African countries of Kenya, Tanzania, and Uganda, where they had suffered intense persecution and threats to their lives as a community. They are Shi'a Muslims and their spiritual leader is His Highness the Aga Khan, who is the forty-ninth hereditary Imam of the Shia Imami Ismaili Muslims and a direct descendant of the Prophet Mohammed through the Prophet's cousin and son-in-law Ali, the first Imam, and his wife, Fatima, the Prophet's daughter. He is the spiritual leader of fourteen million Ismailis living all over the world, mainly in western Central Asia, Africa, the Middle East, Canada, the United States, and western Europe.

The Ismailis integrated into Canadian life through hard work and a belief system that values volunteering in their own community and in the larger society in which they live. Their contribution to Canada's social, political, and economic life has been nothing short of spectacular, including Calgary's Naheed Nenshi, the first Muslim mayor of a major city in North America. Their tradition of volunteerism means they contribute much to the countries where they have spread out in a diaspora. The Aga Khan is known to his people as Mawlana Ḥazar Imam, "Imam of the Time," which means he interprets for them what their faith means in the contemporary world.

Benjamin Constant, "The Liberty of the Ancients Compared with That of the Moderns," in *Political Writings*, translated by Biancamaria Fontana (Cambridge: Cambridge University Press, 1988).

Benjamin Constant, according to the historian François Furet, was obsessed with trying to find an explanation for the insanity that was the Terror in France during 1792. Constant pointed out that the quietest life, the unknown name, offered no protection against the senseless violence instigated and propelled by Saint-Just and Robespierre. He was very close to Madame de Staël, an outstanding writer who was a staunch opponent of Napoleon. The Swiss-French woman with whom I lived when I was learning French in Paris in 1963–64 was a direct descendant of Constant's, and I first read him aloud to her to practise my French diction.

Will Kymlicka, "Education for Citizenship," in *Education in Morality*, edited by Terence McLaughlin and Mark Halstead (London: Routledge, 1999), 85.

All of Kymlicka's writings are important to the academic study of citizenship and should be required reading in every school.

Don DeLillo, *White Noise* (New York: Penguin, 2009), 80–81.

Linda Nguyen, "In Fewer than Two Days, Top Canadian CEOs Earn an Average Worker's Annual Salary," *Globe and Mail*, January 2, 2014, http://www.theglobeandmail.com/report-on-business/careers/in-less-than-two-days-top-canadian-ceos-earn-an-average-workers-annual-salary/article16167343/.

"World Briefing / Europe / France: Heat Toll," *New York Times*, September 26, 2003.

Kelly Tran, Stan Kustec, and Tina Chui, "Becoming Canadian: Intent, Process and Outcome," *Canadian Social Trends* 76 (2005): 9.

For an account of the dynamics of these reforms, see Simon Green, "Much Ado about Not-Very-Much? Assessing Ten Years of German Citizenship Reform," *Citizenship Studies* 16, no. 2 (2012), and Kiran Banerjee, "Toward Post-national Membership? Tensions and Transformation in German and EU Citizenship," *Journal of International Law and International Relations* 10 (2014).

Michael Adams, *Unlikely Utopia: The Surprising Triumph of Canadian Pluralism* (Toronto: Viking Canada, 2007), 82.

Speaking of mixed unions to audiences in Europe will cause an intake of breath. There the idea of racial superiority is very slow to die and haunts and hinders their immigration policies. A very highly placed European official admitted to me that European countries had intentionally chosen illiterate persons from deprived areas of underdeveloped countries as migrant workers so that they would not know their rights and could be shipped home at twenty-four hours' notice. Of course it was understood that they should never become citizens. They are now reaping the benefits of that whirlwind.

Ernest Hemingway, *The Sun Also Rises* (New York: Scribner, 2003), 184–85.

Hemingway is my favourite American writer of the twentieth century, and I consider this novel, which he wrote at the age of twenty-four and published at twenty-six, to be pretty nearly perfect. I possess a first edition of it and treat myself to reading it every two years or so. I know that people read it for the tormented love story and the tangled relationship of the protagonists, but I love it especially for the scenes of fishing where Jake and Bill plumb the streams of mountainous Spain.

George Elliott Clarke, "Guysborough Road Church," in *Saltwater Spirituals and Deeper Blues* (Porters Lake, NS: Pottersfield Press, 1983), 14.

Malcolm Ross, *The Impossible Sum of Our Traditions: Reflections on Canadian Literature* (Toronto: McClelland & Stewart, 1986). The phrase "the impossible sum of our traditions" is borrowed from Robert Kroetsch; see page 201.

Ross, "Our Identity," in *Impossible Sum of Our Traditions*, 25.

I actually liked reading *Our Island Story* and the *Girl's Own Paper* as a child. I hungered for information and thought all information was good. As a colonial product, first of Hong Kong and then of Canada, I learnt a lot about England that I liked and didn't like — it was literate and it rained a lot. This early exposure was confirmed when I visited there, and my opinion has never changed.

Mavis Gallant, "Its Image in the Mirror," in *My Heart Is Broken: Eight Stories and a Short Novel by Mavis Gallant* (New York: Random House, 1964), 89.

Thucydides, quoted in Adrienne Clarkson, "Speech on the Occasion of a Visit to the Canadian Naval Task Group," Halifax, October 15, 2001, http://archive.gg.ca/media/doc.asp?lang=e&DocID=1325.

CHAPTER FOUR: UBUNTU

For me personally, the activism about South Africa was only part of a dynamic time of international interest. We Canadians watched and often participated in the American civil rights movement and the anti–Vietnam War protests, and it was thrilling to accept forty thousand young men who were draft resisters from the United States, all of college age. It was the beginning of the second wave of feminism, starting with publication of Betty Friedan's *The Feminine Mystique* in 1963. To use a quote attributed to Walt Whitman, "O to be alive in such an age, when miracles are everywhere and every inch of common air throbs a tremendous prophecy of greater marvels yet to be."

For a broader discussion of the concept of Ubuntu, see Munyaradzi Felix Murove, "L'Ubuntu," *Diogenes* 235, no. 3 (2011): 44.

Stephen Theron, *Africa, Philosophy and the Western Tradition: An Essay in Self-Understanding* (Frankfurt: Peter Lang, 1995), 35.

When I first heard Roméo Dallaire talk about human beings in this way, I understood why his conscientiousness had led to a nervous breakdown after the genocide in Rwanda. His continued activity and advocacy in areas such as the fight against child soldiers is an inspiration; he continues to apply his considerable energy and spiritual resources to these questions despite his fragility.

Voltaire, *Letters on England*, translated by L. Tancock (Harmondsworth, UK: Penguin, 1980), 41.

Broadbent Institute, "Canadian Values Are Progressive Values: A Snapshot of the Views of New and Canadian-Born Urban/Suburban Canadians, 2013," Ottawa: Broadbent Institute, 2013.

Georges Erasmus, "The LaFontaine-Baldwin Lecture 2002," in *The LaFontaine-Baldwin Lectures, Volume One: A Dialogue on Democracy in Canada*, edited by Rudyard Griffiths (Toronto: Penguin Canada, 2002).

The line is from Terence's *Heauton Timorumenos* (The Self-Tormentor), written in 163 BCE. I have to admit that I have never read a single one of Terence's plays, and the only line of his I know is the one I have quoted. This line and Akira Kurosawa's "The artist never averts his eyes" are, to my mind, the two lines you should repeat to yourself if you ever hope to have a relationship with another human being or to create anything.

Michael Oakeshott, "On Being Conservative," in *Rationalism in Politics and Other Essays* (London: Methuen, 1962), 177.

D. G. Jones, *Butterfly on Rock: Study of Themes and Images in Canadian Literature* (Toronto: University of Toronto Press, 1970), 5.

Jürgen Habermas, "Citizenship and National Identity: Some Reflections on the Future of Europe," *Praxis International* 12 (1992): 7.

CHAPTER FIVE: GROSS NATIONAL HAPPINESS

Northrop Frye, quoted in Adrienne Clarkson, *Room for All of Us: Surprising Stories of Loss and Transformation* (Toronto: Allen Lane Canada, 2011), 15.

I took Northrop Frye's course "The Anatomy of Criticism" in graduate school at the University of Toronto in 1961. The brilliance of his analysis was matched by a generosity of spirit in dealing with students.

He looked at the thirty of us with a level determination that only the very shy exhibit. He was head of the Department of English when I became a lecturer the next year at Victoria College. We had one particularly memorable conversation when I blurted out that I thought an academic career was really not in the cards for me. He concurred monosyllabically, but in the kindest possible way.

Hans Vaihinger, *The Philosophy of "As If": A System of the Theoretical, Practical and Religious Fictions of Mankind*, translated by C. K. Ogden (New York: Harcourt, Brace, 1935).

In studying for my fourth-year honours exams in English-language literature, I set myself to reading through the whole of *The Literary History of England* by Baugh, Brooke, Chew, and Sherbourne, one hour every day, plus the other material for my courses in Victorian poetry, etc., etc. One night I looked up with glazed eyes and saw on the shelf *The Philosophy of "As If,"* by Hans Vaihinger. I had taken philosophy for four years and never heard of him. Learning that he was a follower of Kant, about whom I would also be doing an exam, I drew him from the shelf. I was hooked. The only other person who ever shared my enthusiasm for Vaihinger was a life insurance agent I talked to once. How the subject came up, I don't remember.

Friedrich Carl Forbergs, quoted in Vaihinger, *Philosophy of "As If,"* 322–23, 325.

Citizenship in the European countries is a label of expectations imposed on the citizen. What we have succeeded in doing in Canada is define our country by what we are and what we bring to it.

Farley Mowat, *Never Cry Wolf* (Toronto: Emblem, 2009).

H. L. Mencken, "Philosophers as Liars," *American Mercury* 3, no.10 (October 1924): 253–55.

Karma Ura and Karma Galay, *Gross National Happiness and Development* (Thimphu: Centre for Bhutan Studies, 2004).

Archery matches celebrate every major state visit or event in Bhutan. On one notable occasion — the coronation of the present king's father — the American representative, Senator Daniel Moynihan, was shot through the foot by an unfocused arrow. We were cautioned to stand well back.

Aristotle, *Aristotle's Nicomachean Ethics*, translated by Robert C. Bartlett and Susan D. Collins (Chicago: University of Chicago Press, 2011), 23: 1102a–5.

Aristotle, *The Nicomachean Ethics of Aristotle*, translated by Robert Williams (London: Longmans Green, 1869), 23: 1100a–10.

Aristotle, *Nicomachean Ethics* (trans. Bartlett and Collins), 5: 1095a–20.

Even if honour is forgotten in our public life, we should still acknowledge the concept. One of the best literary examples of honour is in the play *Minna von Barnhelm*, by Gotthold Lessing, written in 1767 at the end of the Seven Years' War. I saw it in a brilliant production by Giorgio Strehler thirty years ago at the Théâtre de l'Europe; it made the concept of honour seem emotionally real and touchingly absurd without detracting from the worth of the concept.

Malcolm Ross, *The Impossible Sum of Our Traditions: Reflections on Canadian Literature* (Toronto: McClelland & Stewart, 1986).

Auditor General of Canada, "Programs for First Nations on Reserves," chapter 4 of *Status Report of the Auditor General of Canada to the House of Commons* (Ottawa: Office of the Auditor General of Canada, 2011).

In *A Fair Country*, John Ralston Saul puts forth this seminal idea of our indebtedness to the Aboriginal and Métis peoples in a definitive and imaginative way. See *A Fair Country: Telling Truths about Canada* (Toronto: Viking Canada, 2008).

Hannah Arendt, *The Human Condition* (Chicago: University of Chicago Press, 1998), 241.

Charles Taylor, *Reconciling the Solitudes: Essays on Canadian Federalism and Nationalism* (Montreal: McGill-Queen's University Press, 1993), 190.

Nancy Strickland has been a remarkable Canadian presence in Bhutan for many years. Her energy and commitment to this unique country have helped me understand it more deeply. She is an example of how one person can make a difference in our relationship with another country.

Aristotle, *Physics*, 3.4: 293b, quoted in Adrienne Clarkson, "Making Migrants Part of Society: The Canadian Experience," presentation to the Conference on Integration of Immigration, Brussels, November 25, 2003, http://archive.gg.ca/media/doc.asp?lang=e&DocID=4067.

Grand Chief John Kelly, "We Are All in the Ojibway Circle" (testimony before the Royal Commission on the Northern Environment, 1977), in *From Ink Lake: Canadian Stories Selected by Michael Ondaatje*, edited by Michael Ondaatje, 579–91 (Toronto: Vintage Canada, 1995).

BIBLIOGRAPHY

Adams, Michael. *Unlikely Utopia : The Surprising Triumph of Canadian Pluralism*. Toronto: Viking Canada, 2007.

Aga Kahn. "Lecture by His Highness the Aga Khan: The LaFontaine-Baldwin Lecture (Toronto, Canada)." October 15, 2010. http://www.akdn.org/Content/1018.

Arendt, Hannah. *The Human Condition*. Chicago: University of Chicago Press, 1998.

Aristotle. *Aristotle's Nicomachean Ethics*. Translated by Robert C. Bartlett and Susan D. Collins. Chicago: University of Chicago Press, 2011.

———. *The Nicomachean Ethics of Aristotle*. Translated by Robert Williams. London: Longmans, Green, 1869.

———. *Politics*. Translated by Ernest Barker. Edited by R. F. Stalley. Oxford: Oxford University Press, 1995.

Atherton, Gertrude. *The Immortal Marriage*. New York: Boni and Liveright, 1927.

Auditor General of Canada. "Programs for First Nations on Reserves." Chapter 4 of *Status Report of the Auditor General of Canada to the House of Commons*. Ottawa: Office of the Auditor General of Canada, 2011.

Balot, Ryan K. *Greek Political Thought*. Toronto: Wiley, 2008.

Banerjee, Kiran. "Toward Post-national Membership? Tensions and Transformation in German and EU Citizenship." *Journal of International Law and International Relations* 9, no. 3 (2014).

Berlin, Isaiah. *Four Essays on Liberty*. Oxford: Oxford University Press, 1969.

Bloch, Marc. *Feudal Society*. Translated by L. A. Manyon. London: Routledge & Kegan Paul, 1961.

Broadbent Institute. "Canadian Values Are Progressive Values: A Snapshot of the Views of New and Canadian-Born Urban/Suburban Canadians, 2013." Ottawa: Broadbent Institute, 2013.

Burke, Edmund. *Edmund Burke: Further Reflections on the Revolution in France*. Edited by Daniel E. Ritchie. Indianapolis: Liberty Fund, 1992.

———. *Reflections on the Revolution in France*. Edited by Frank M. Turner. New Haven, CT: Yale University Press, 2003.

———. *Select Works of Edmund Burke: A New Imprint of the Payne Edition*. Vol. 4. Indianapolis: Liberty Fund, 1999.

Byock, Jesse. "The Icelandic Althing: Dawn of Parliamentary Democracy." In *Heritage and Identity: Shaping the Nations of the North*, edited by J. M. Fladmark. Shaftesbury, UK: Donhead, 2002.

Clarke, George Elliott. "Guysborough Road Church." In *Saltwater Spirituals and Deeper Blues*. Porters Lake, NS: Pottersfield Press, 1983.

Clarkson, Adrienne. "Making Migrants Part of Society: The Canadian Experience." Presentation to Conference on Integration of Immigration, Brussels, November 25, 2003. http://archive.gg.ca/media/doc.asp?lang=e&DocID=4067.

———. *Room for All of Us: Surprising Stories of Loss and Transformation*. Toronto: Allen Lane Canada, 2011.

———. "Speech on the Occasion of a Visit to the Canadian Naval Task Group." Delivered in Halifax, NS, October 15, 2001. http://archive.gg.ca/media/doc.asp?lang=e&DocID=1325.

Constant, Benjamin. *Political Writings*. Translated by Biancamaria Fontana. Cambridge: Cambridge University Press, 1988.

Coulton, G. G. *From St. Francis to Dante: Translations from the Chronicle of the Franciscan Salimbene, 1221–1288*. London: Nutt, 1907.

Daftary, Farhad (ed.). *A Modern History of the Ismailis: Continuity and Change in a Muslim Community*. Canada: Palgrave Macmillan, 2011.

Davis, Natalie Zemon. *The Return of Martin Guerre*. Cambridge, MA: Harvard University Press, 1983.

DeLillo, Don. *White Noise*. New York: Penguin, 2009.

Durrell, Lawrence. *Caesar's Vast Ghost: Aspects of Provence*. New York: Faber & Faber, 2002.

Erasmus, Georges. "The LaFontaine-Baldwin Lecture 2002." In *The LaFontaine-Baldwin Lectures, Volume One: A Dialogue on Democracy in Canada*. Edited by Rudyard Griffiths. Toronto: Penguin Canada, 2002.

Fitzgerald, F. Scott. *The Crack-Up*. Edited by Edmund Wilson. New York: New Directions, 1993.

Frost, Robert. *The Letters of Robert Frost to Louis Untermeyer*. New York: Holt, Rinehart and Winston, 1963.

Gallant, Mavis. "Its Image in the Mirror." In *My Heart Is Broken: Eight Stories and a Short Novel by Mavis Gallant*. New York: Random House, 1964.

Gildea, Robert. *Children of the Revolution: The French, 1799–1914*. London: Penguin Group, 2008.

Green, Simon. "Much Ado about Not-Very-Much? Assessing Ten Years of German Citizenship Reform." *Citizenship Studies* 16, no. 2 (2012).

Habermas, Jürgen. "Citizenship and National Identity: Some Reflections on the Future of Europe". *Praxis International* 12 (1992).

Hemingway, Ernest. *The Sun Also Rises*. New York: Scribner, 2003.

Herodotus. *The Landmark Herodotus: The Histories*. Edited by Robert B. Strassler. Translated by Andrea Purvis. New York: Random House, 2007.

James, Henry, and Richard Howard. *Collected Travel Writings*. New York: Library of America, 1993.

Jones, D. G. *Butterfly on Rock: Study of Themes and Images in Canadian Literature*. Toronto: University of Toronto Press, 1970.

Jung, Carl. *Collected Works*. Translated by R. F. C. Hull. Princeton, NJ: Bollingen, 1976.

Kelly, John. "We Are All in the Ojibway Circle." In *From Ink Lake: Canadian Stories Selected by Michael Ondaatje*, edited by Michael Ondaatje, 579–91. Toronto: Vintage Canada, 1995.

Kraut, Richard. "Citizenship in Aristotle's Politics." In *Aristotle's Politics: Critical Essays*, edited by Richard Kraut and Steven Skultety. Rowman & Littlefield, 2005.

Kymlicka, Will. "Education for Citizenship." In *Education in Morality*, edited by Terence McLaughlin and Mark Halstead. London: Routledge, 1999.

Laurence, Margaret. "My Final Hour." Address to Trent Seminary, Mississauga, ON, March 29, 1983. Reprinted as "My Final Hour." *Canadian Literature* 100, (Spring 1984).

———. *The Prophet's Camel Bell*. Toronto: McClelland and Stewart, 1963.

Lewis, Thomas. *The Lives of a Cell: Notes of a Biology Watcher*. New York: Viking, 1974.

Lewis, Thomas, Fari Amini, and Richard Lannon. *A General Theory of Love*. New York: Random House, 2000.

McCarthy, Mary. "The Man in the Brooks Brothers Shirt." In *The Company She Keeps*. New York: Harcourt, Brace, 1942.

Mencken, H. L. "Philosophers as Liars." *The American Mercury* 3, no.10 (October 1924).

Mill, John Stuart. *On Liberty, the Subjection of Women, and Utilitarianism*. Toronto: Random House, 2002.

Mowat, Farley. *Never Cry Wolf*. Toronto: Emblem, 2009.

Murove, Munyaradzi Felix. "L'Ubuntu." *Diogenes* 235, no. 3 (2011): 44.

Nanji, Azim. "The Nizami Ismaili Commnity in North America." *The Muslim Community in North America*. Ed. Earle H. Waugh. Alberta: University of Alberta Press, 1983.

Nguyen, Linda. "In Fewer than Two Days, Top Canadian CEOs Earn an Average Worker's Annual Salary." *Globe and Mail*, January 2, 2014. http://www.theglobeandmail.com/report-on-business/careers/in-less-than-two-days-top-canadian-ceos-earn-an-average-workers-annual-salary/article16167343/.

Oakeshott, Michael. *Rationalism in Politics and Other essays*. London: Methuen, 1962.

Pezet, Maurice. *Les Alpilles*. Paris: Horizons de France, 1955.

Raaflaub, Kurt A. "The Breakthrough of Demokratia in Mid-Fifth-Century Athens." In *Origins of Democracy in Ancient Greece*, 105–54. Berkeley: University of California Press, 2007.

———. "Contemporary Perceptions of Democracy in Fifth-Century Athens." *Classica et Mediaevalia* 40 (1989): 33–70.

Ross, Malcolm. *The Impossible Sum of Our Traditions: Reflections on Canadian Literature*. Toronto: McClelland & Stewart, 1986.

Saul, John Ralston. *A Fair Country: Telling Truths about Canada*. Toronto: Viking Canada, 2008.

Segal, Hugh. "Toward a New Definition of Citizenship: Beneath and Beyond the Nation-State." *The Dynamics of Decentralization: Canadian Federalism and British Devolution*. Eds. Trevor C. Salmon and Michael Keating. Montreal: McGill-Queen's University Press, 2001: 175–185

Smith, Rogers M. *Stories of Peoplehood: The Politics and Morals of Political Membership*. Cambridge: Cambridge University Press, 2003.

Taylor, Charles. *Reconciling the Solitudes: Essays on Canadian Federalism and Nationalism*. Montreal: McGill-Queen's University Press, 1993.

Theron, Stephen. *Africa, Philosophy and the Western Tradition: An Essay in Self-Understanding*. Frankfurt: Peter Lang, 1995.

Thucydides. *History of the Peloponnesian War*. Translated by Rex Warner. Baltimore, MD: Penguin Books, 1972.

———. *The Landmark Thucydides: A Comprehensive Guide to the Peloponnesian War*. Edited by Robert B. Strassler. Translated by Richard Crawley. New York: Random House, 2008.

Tocqueville, Alexis de. *Democracy in America*. Translated by Harvey C. Mansfield and Debra Winthrop. Chicago: University of Chicago Press, 2000.

Tran, Kelly, Stan Kustec, and Tina Chui. "Becoming Canadian: Intent, Process and Outcome." *Canadian Social Trends* 76 (2005).

Turnbull, Colin. *The Mountain People*. New York: Simon & Schuster, 1987.

Turnbull, Colin, Colin Higgins, and Denis Cannan. *The Ik*. Woodstock, IL: Dramatic Publishing, 1985.

Ura, Karma, and Karma Galay. *Gross National Happiness and Development*. Thimphu: Centre for Bhutan Studies, 2004.

Vaihinger, Hans. *The Philosophy of "As If": A System of the Theoretical, Practical and Religious Fictions of Mankind*. Translated by C. K. Ogden. New York: Harcourt, Brace, 1935

Voltaire. *Letters on England*. Translated by L. Tancock. Harmondsworth, UK: Penguin, 1980.

Walzer, Michael. *Spheres of Justice*. New York: Basic Books, 1983.

"World Briefing / Europe / France: Heat Toll." *New York Times*, September 26, 2003.

PERMISSIONS

Permission is gratefully acknowledged to reprint the excerpt from the poem titled "Guysborough Road Church," by George Elliott Clarke, on page 107. The poem was published originally in *Saltwater Spirituals and Deeper Blues* (Porters Lake, NS: Pottersfield Press, 1983). Permission granted by the author.

ACKNOWLEDGEMENTS

I HAVE BEEN DEVOTED to the Massey Lectures as a listener and reader since Barbara Ward delivered *The Rich Nations and The Poor Nations* in 1961. I marvelled then that a woman should be the first to give these lectures named for Vincent Massey. I still do. And her lectures are among the finest in this series.

I am delighted and honoured to be part of the Massey Lecturers, all of whom have been concerned with the common good. When the subject of citizenship was proposed as the theme, I was enthusiastic as belonging is the subject of my existence.

CBC Radio has been part of my life since I was eight years old, when I received a maroon Bakelite radio for my birthday with which I could listen to CBC Radio's *Stage 47* (and subsequently *48*, *49*, etc.) and the Metropolitan Opera broadcasts on Saturday afternoons. Although my career spanned thirty-five years in CBC Television, this is the first broadcast that I have ever done for CBC Radio, apart from being interviewed sporadically. I love the sound of the human voice on radio. I think it is fitting that after all these years I should return to my first true love.

These lectures were never intended to be academic. They were meant to appeal to the largest possible audience who have the machinery with which to hear them, both in their brains and on the radio. The essence of public broadcasting is that it must give to the public a voice for the ideas which circulate in our country and which make us a people. The CBC has always done this, and CBC Radio in particular has succeeded in this respect with distinction. In these lectures I feel that I am communicating directly with the people among whom I live and that it is a part of an ongoing conversation. I don't consider the lectures to be a one-way street. All of broadcasting, as I learned over a long career, is full of expectation of engaged reception and full of hope about stimulating lively dialogue.

There are many people to thank for the help that they have given me in so many different ways. I owe an enormous debt to Philip Coulter, a most extraordinary producer of radio documentaries, a person of high intelligence and deep sensitivity who shares my devotion to Stompin' Tom Connors. To Janie Yoon, a very skilful editor who combines equal parts of scalpel and soft-soap in one engaging personality. To John Fraser, who has just finished a remarkable tenure as Master of Massey College, for his support, encouragement, and kindness. To the extraordinary Bernie Lucht who has presided over twenty-eight lectures and to Greg Kelly, both of whom know what it means to bear the responsibilities of being an executive producer at the CBC, this specialized and rather arcane knowledge I happen to share and therefore appreciate profoundly. To Heather Conway and Chris Boyce, who understood immediately what these lectures represent.

To my assistant Aidan Denison who makes everything happen when it should. For his meticulous and enthusiastic research, many thanks to Kiran Banerjee. To Gillian Smith and all the staff at the Institute for Canadian Citizenship for their hard work and efforts to bring my dreams about Canadian citizenship into reality. Thanks to Natalie Zemon Davis for her example, her scholarship. To Andrew Griffith for his advice and friendship. To

Micheline Steals for her excellent skills and Michael Levine for his unfailing support.

Many thanks to Scott and Krystyne Griffin, the extraordinary couple whose love of poetry and literature has changed the intellectual climate of this country — he with his determination and imaginative creation of the Griffin Poetry Prize, and she with her magnificent elegant energy in helping with the enterprise. I only wish they had come onto the Canadian literary scene decades ago! The Griffin tenure at House of Anansi has made all the difference to us in Canada. To Sarah MacLachlan and the staff at Anansi who are committed and enthusiastic.

And to John who is always present.

Vincent Massey, as the first Canadian Governor General and as thinker, philanthropist, and political figure, made an immeasurable contribution to the culture and independence of this country. Flying over the North Pole in 1956 in a Twin Otter, he released a small canister containing a piece of paper declaring, "This is Canada."

INDEX

(THE CBC MASSEY LECTURES SERIES)

Blood
Lawrence Hill
978-1-77089-322-1 (p)

The Universe Within
Neil Turok
978-1-77089-015-2 (p)

Winter
Adam Gopnik
978-0-88784-974-9 (p)

Player One
Douglas Coupland
978-0-88784-972-5 (p)

The Wayfinders
Wade Davis
978-0-88784-842-1 (p)

Payback
Margaret Atwood
978-0-88784-810-0 (p)

More Lost Massey Lectures
Bernie Lucht, ed.
978-0-88784-801-8 (p)

The City of Words
Alberto Manguel
978-0-88784-763-9 (p)

The Lost Massey Lectures
Bernie Lucht, ed.
978-0-88784-217-7 (p)

The Ethical Imagination
Margaret Somerville
978-0-88784-747-9 (p)

Race Against Time
Stephen Lewis
978-0-88784-753-0 (p)

A Short History of Progress
Ronald Wright
978-0-88784-706-6 (p)

The Truth About Stories
Thomas King
978-0-88784-696-0 (p)

Beyond Fate
Margaret Visser
978-0-88784-679-3 (p)

LOVE THE MASSEY LECTURES? THERE'S AN APP FOR THAT!

Available for free on the iTunes App Store, the award-winning Massey Lectures iPad App immerses users in the Massey universe. Winner of the Silver Cannes Lion award for Digital Online Design, the app brings together, for the first time, the full text of the CBC Massey Lectures with the audio recordings of the live lectures, and contains free bonus content, including discussions, related articles, video interviews, and more.

Uncover the full legacy and history of the CBC Massey Lectures Series, from 1961 to today. Learn more about selected Massey authors, their lives, their achievements, and their beliefs. Explore the complex web of themes within the Massey universe, and hear unique thoughts and insights from the lecturers. And contribute to the conversation yourself.

Download at bit.ly/MasseysApp

MASSEY LECTURES   ANANSI

The Massey Lectures iPad App was conceived, designed, and developed by Critical Mass, a global digital marketing agency.